Contents

List of boxes, figures and tables

Acknowledgements

We should like to thank the Joseph Rowntree Foundation for its support and, in particular, the Foundation's Director Richard Best, whose idea it was, and Peter Marcus the Policy and Practice Development Manager. The contribution made by the Project Advisory Group members was outstanding and we should like to record our thanks to them:

Dr. Mary-Lee Athorn BWB Partnership, Nottingham and Chair of the BURA working party on contaminated land.

Edward Cooke Head of Planning and Development, TLT Solicitors, Bristol and a member of the United Kingdom Environmental Law Association

Peter Giles Deputy Director of Housing Operations (Property Services), Joseph Rowntree Housing Trust, York

Joanne Kwan Research Manager - contaminated land, Construction Industry Research and Information Association (CIRIA)

Dr. Paul Nathanail Course Director, MSc Contaminated Land Management, LQM, University of Nottingham, member of FOCIL

Alex Ritchie NHBC Engineer (contaminated land), National House Building Council (NHBC)

Harry Shipley Chairman of the National Land Reclamation Panel and Major Projects Manager for Gateshead MBC

During the course of the research we interviewed or contacted a great many people in connection with the case studies themselves, for background research and in respect of developments that were not included in the final report. We should like to record our thanks to all concerned for their time and assistance.

Paul Syms
Peter Knight
School of Environment and Development
Sheffield Hallam University
August 2000

Executive Summary

This research forms part of the Joseph Rowntree Foundation's 'policies into practice' programme and examines problems associated with developing previously used land. The study relates to two Government policies, the remediation of land affected by contamination and the reuse of previously-developed land for housing purposes.

The experiences of housing developers are used to illustrate the redevelopment process and highlight some of the problems faced by developers when tackling 'previously-developed' land. The research examined ten case studies of sites previously used for differing purposes and where various methods were employed for site remediation. The developments include social housing, shared ownership tenure, apartments and executive homes.

The study takes a constructive approach to the redevelopment process and does not seek to single out examples of 'bad practice' or avoidable mistakes. The case studies provide a number of useful lessons for housing developers and their advisors but there are four over-arching lessons applicable to all redevelopment situations:

- **the need for a comprehensive site investigation, of which the historic study of land use forms an essential part;**

- **the need for a comprehensive written and photographic record, including waste handling notes, of all remediation works;**

- **the need for validation to demonstrate compliance with the remediation strategy and achievement of its goals;**

- **the need for factually correct and readily assimilated information on past uses, site investigations and remediation works to be made available to purchasers and tenants.**

Assessing and treating development land

Before purchasing a site developers should employ a suitably qualified consultant to undertake a preliminary assessment to identify any possible hazards that may affect development. A desk study involves collection and analysis of available data and a walkover survey is an inspection of the site and surrounding area using information from the desk study. Together, these allow the consultant to characterise the site and assess its suitability for housing development.

The preliminary site assessment will identify parts of the site where there may be the possibility of contamination and highlight areas for intrusive investigation. No ground investigation can guarantee to locate all contaminants that may exist within a site. The objective of an investigation should be to assess, with a reasonable degree of certainty, the likelihood of any contamination being present, the nature of the contaminants themselves and the media in which they are located.

Site investigation reports should be non-technical so that they may be understood by the developer and appropriate regulatory authorities. They should include information relating to the site history, sampling strategy, analysis of results, maps showing trial-pit and bore-hole locations, site profiles, remediation strategies and a set of summary conclusions.

Various options exist for the remediation of different types of contamination. These include:

• **Excavation and disposal**

• **Containment (in-situ or ex-situ)**

• **Soil Treatment Methods**

The selection of the most appropriate options will often have a significant impact on the viability of a housing development.

The case studies

Ten development sites were studied, eight where development had been completed or was underway, one where work had not commenced and one where the intending developer had abandoned the project. The sites previously had been used for many different purposes:

• **Brickworks, Shallow mine workings, Road haulage, Made ground:**

• **Cotton mill, bleach works, oil seals manufacture:**

• **Dye works, chemical works, railway, cattle pens, coal merchants, electric lightbulb manufacture, oil depot and scrap yard:**

• **Iron works, lime kiln dock, timber yard, town gas works:**

• **Landfill:**

- Petrol filling station and motor vehicle workshops:

- Rail yard forming part of a town gas works:

- Road haulage:

- Shipbuilding works:

- Timber mill:

Conclusions and recommendations

Eleven distinct phases of development were identified and the main conclusions and recommendations for each were:

Project inception - developers and regulators must be prepared to act in a flexible manner to achieve the redevelopment of 'previously used' or 'brownfield' land and buildings.

Site acquisition and site assembly - landowners may have completely unrealistic ideas about the value of their land but, equally, they may be trapped by historic valuations and the fact that the land is used as collateral against bank borrowings or other loans.

Site assessment - it is important to identify any access or site constraints, including the adequacy of infrastructure, which may affect the development. All site assessments must initially comprise of an historical study followed by a 'walkover' survey.

Contaminant (Source) -pathway-receptor - all possible linkages should be considered. Remember that it may not be necessary to remove all contamination from the site, it may be feasible to break or remove the pathway instead.

Detailed design - examine the layout of the site and be prepared to consider alternative remediation strategies given different layouts.

Feasibility study - having completed the site assessment and having identified all potential pollutant linkages, the revised design should be the subject of a comprehensive review.

Planning and regulatory approvals - close liaison with the regulators during the earlier phases should ensure that the necessary information has been collected and can be presented in support of the applications. The need, or otherwise, for Waste Management or Mobile Plant licences should be identified as early as possible.

Development finance - banks and other financial institutions are probably more prepared to provide development finance for 'previously used' sites than they were a few years ago, but there are still a few exceptions. Possible sources of grant aid should be identified and negotiations commenced as soon as possible after project inception.

Tendering - the appointment of contractors with experience of site remediation can be beneficial, as they may be able to suggest ways of undertaking the work. The scope of the work should be adequately described.

Construction - the site remediation/preparation works must be properly supervised and, most importantly, must be fully recorded - ideally this will involve maintaining photographic and written records, including sketches of where contaminants, or other site constraints such as old services, were located.

Sales and marketing - this includes the communication of information, to prospective purchasers and tenants, as to the previous use of the site, the contaminants found and the methods employed to prepare the site for redevelopment. It is important to be open with information relating to the site and its development, as any attempt at concealment is likely to have an adverse effect once it is discovered.

1. Introduction

An earlier research report *The Redevelopment of Contaminated Land for Housing Use* (Syms, 1997) considered many of the obstacles faced by housebuilders (both private and social developers) when considering the redevelopment of previously used and contaminated land. The study was supported by the Joseph Rowntree Foundation and also investigated the perceptions of members of the public, as potential house buyers and tenants. It asked whether or not they would be prepared to live in homes constructed on previously contaminated sites and found that potential occupiers wished to be informed about site histories and remediation measures.

The report made a number of recommendations to the housing development industry and to government, many of which have now been adopted by individual housebuilders, the National House-Builders Council (NHBC) and by government.

Included in the previous study were several brief case studies, used to highlight some of the issues and to formulate recommendations. The Joseph Rowntree Foundation felt that, as part of its 'policies into practice' programme, it would be useful to examine in greater depth some of the problems confronting the developers of previously used land and commissioned the research team to undertake a further study. The study relates directly to two important Government policies, the remediation of land affected by contamination and the reuse of previously used land for housing purposes.

The experiences of housing developers are used to illustrate the redevelopment process and highlight some of the problems faced by developers when tackling 'previously used' land. It examines a further ten case studies in greater detail than the previous report. The studies are geographically distributed throughout England, the sites were previously used for differing purposes and various methods were employed for site remediation. The new developments include social housing, shared ownership tenure, apartments and executive homes.

In selecting the case studies the authors were conscious of the drawbacks associated with this type of study. Some case studies can be repetitious, whilst others may be unrepresentative of situations found in practice. They can also become out of date in a relatively short period of time. The developments used in this study have therefore been selected with great care, to illustrate many different situations in terms of previous land uses, remediation methods employed and the types of housing developments undertaken. Health and Safety issues and Construction Design Management are outside the scope of this study, except where specifically referred to in the case studies. Reference should be made to published guidance and regulations in these areas.

The authors were fortunate to have the support of an excellent advisory group, whose members included representatives from NHBC and Construction Industry Research and Information Association (CIRIA), as well as the professions involved in the redevelopment process. One of the greatest problems faced by the authors and the advisory group was deciding what information to include and what could be excluded from each of the case studies. A great deal of information was obtained for each of the studied developments, sufficient perhaps to write a full research report on each, but that was not the objective of this report. Some limits had to be imposed on the length of each chapter and, for some readers; greater levels of detail may have been desirable. Whilst recognising this we took the decision to include the information that was considered to be of greatest interest to the widest range of readers.

The study examines ten housing developments, some were already completed at the time of the research, on others development was in progress, one site where work on site had not yet started and one where the project had been abandoned by the developer. Many other developments were considered but were considered not to be appropriate for inclusion.

For the most part we received friendly co-operation from the housing developers, the consultants and the local authorities. One developer, of a housing estate where problems had been experienced, refused to assist the study for fear that further adverse publicity would be attracted. A small number of developers, when invited to participate, declined to become involved for fear that something detrimental may be discovered, or for reasons of commercial confidentiality - not wishing to share their experiences with others.

A few, potentiality interesting, cases could not be used because they were the subject of litigation or contractural disputes. These included allegations of misrepresentation, in terms of the information provided to purchasers, and inadequacies in information provided to contractors for use in tendering. Other developments were omitted because they either duplicated the lessons in selected studies, or added little to the overall report.

The intention has been to take a constructive, and helpful, approach to the redevelopment process, not to single out examples of 'bad practice' or avoidable mistakes. The case studies described in chapters four to thirteen provide a number of useful lessons for housing developers and their advisors but there are four over-arching lessons applicable to all redevelopment situations:

- **the need for a comprehensive site investigation, of which the historic study of land use forms an essential part;**

- the need for a comprehensive written and photographic record, including waste handling notes, of all remediation works;

- the need for validation to demonstrate compliance with the strategy and achievement of the remediation goals;

- the need for factually correct and readily assimilated information on past uses, site investigations and remediation works to be made available to purchasers and tenants.

Structure of the report

The rest of this chapter provides an overview of the redevelopment process. Chapter two addresses the policy background and considers the site assembly, town planning, environmental, legal and sales problems associated with redevelopment. Chapter three provides a brief overview of the technical problems and solutions.

Chapters four to thirteen contain the case studies, with the historic uses providing the chapter title, the remediation methods and type of housing forming sub-titles. The principal historic use of the case study site is listed first, as the chapter title, with the remediation method(s) and type(s) of housing development forming sub-titles. Chapter fourteen draws together the lessons to be learned from the case studies.

At the end of each case study chapter, the issues identified are commented upon by the authors and key points are listed. Reference is also made to the relevant Industry Profiles in the series published by the DETR, which provide details of industrial activities, the ways in which ground contamination may be caused and the contaminants associated with the different land uses. Similar information, in an abbreviated form, may also be found in the *Desk Reference Guide to potentially Contaminative Land Uses* (Syms, 1999).

The redevelopment process

The 'recycling' of land is nothing new, it has been going on in the United Kingdom, and other industrialised nations, for decades and in some locations even for centuries. Buildings have reached the end of their physical or economic lifecycles and have been 'torn down', to be replaced with structures meeting the requirements of new generations. Very often the land uses have undergone significant changes, which can be plotted by reference to old maps.

What has changed in the last two decades is the evolvement of a greater awareness of the implications for redevelopment posed by the presence of contamination in the land. Initially perceived as being 'something to be dealt with by the engineers', usually in the context of excavating the contaminated material and disposing of it in a landfill, the implications of dealing with contamination are now much more widely recognised by developers and their advisers.

The redevelopment process specifically applied to land affected by the presence of contamination may be seen as consisting of eleven phases, many of which are interdependent upon each other. These phases comprise:

- **project inception** - the initial idea, site identification, preliminary design, tentative demand studies, initial costs and development appraisals etc.;

- **site acquisition and site assembly** - relatively straightforward if it is a single site that is being actively marketed but becoming more complex with increasing numbers of ownerships and interests - requiring carefully negotiated options and conditional contracts;

- **site assessment** - the investigation phase, to determine whether or not the site is contaminated and, if so, the extent to which it may affect the development - also includes assessment of available service infrastructures;

- **contaminant-pathway-receptor** analysis and reporting - should include recommendations as to remediation strategy;

- **detailed design** - reworking the original ideas to take account of discovered ground conditions and other possible constraints, such as the inability to acquire, or redevelop, the entire site;

- **feasibility study** - review of detailed design and costs, comprehensive demand studies;

- **planning and regulatory approvals** - remediation of soil contamination through the planning process may involve the need to satisfy both the council's environmental health department and the Environment Agency as well as the planning officers;

- **land and development finance** - identifying appropriate sources, including possible partners (e.g. sources of grant aid) and negotiating funds;

- **tendering** - selection of suitable contractors, single or multiple contracts (e.g. site remediation, infrastructure, construction), form of contract, tendering process, contract documentation etc.;

- **construction** - including site remediation, monitoring and auditing, site infrastructure, construction, landscaping etc.;

- **sales and marketing** - to include communication of information regarding site history, site investigations and remediation works.

The same phases of redevelopment apply regardless of whether the intending developer is a private house builder, a housing association or a public authority, although the emphasis on the individual phases may differ. Most private sector developers will be prepared to commit some money towards demand studies and preliminary designs but will be wary of entering into firm commitments to purchase land without full information as to its condition. On the other hand, it is possible that public authorities and housing associations may be driven more by a need to fulfil a social requirement, or to provide housing in a particular area of demand, and thereby be less concerned about the state of the land.

Through the site assessment, detailed design and feasibility study phases developers need to maintain a degree of flexibility regarding their redevelopment proposals. They should be prepared to 'rethink' the nature of the development in the light of information obtained. For example, it may transpire that the soil conditions are such that, without extensive remediation, the site is not suitable for housing with private gardens (in which vegetables may be grown and children will play) but may be acceptable for low to medium rise flats with mainly 'hard' landscaping. The developer is then faced with the choice of either changing the scheme or incurring additional remediation costs - with both options possibly necessitating a renegotiation of the purchase price. The landowner, however, may not be in a position to renegotiate, requiring a certain sum of money to repay borrowings or to facilitate relocation of a manufacturing operation.

Government policy is that most contamination arising through the historic use of land should be dealt with through the planning system. This applies except where 'significant harm' is being or is likely to be caused, or pollution of controlled waters is being, or is likely to be caused, in which case the regulators (local authorities and the Environment Agency) may take action unconnected to the planning regime. Intending developers need to recognise that the regulators may have different agendas regarding a single site. In one of the case studies described in the previous research (Syms, 1997) the Environment Agency was satisfied with the developer's proposals in terms of waste management procedures but the local authority's environmental health department had concerns over noise, dust and smell from the remediation works.

Whilst banks, building societies and other financial institutions may recognise the need to recycle land as part of the urban regeneration process, they may be less than willing to commit their investors' money to the process. In some cases they may be open to convincing but in others they may be firmly set against funding the development of housing on previously contaminated land. Nevertheless, there are many financial institutions willing and able to support this type of project.

The selection of suitably experienced contractors is extremely important, especially if new, or relatively untried, forms of site remediation are to be employed. Whilst 'fixed price' forms of contract may be desirable to the developer, they may result in higher tender prices or be unacceptable to the contractor. Some form of 'cost over-run' insurance may be a solution acceptable to both developer and contractor, but it is possible that the amount of information required by the insurer will be similar to that demanded by a contractor invited to enter into a 'fixed price' form of contract.

Regardless of their objectives, whether they be profits for shareholders or the provision of social housing in areas of deprivation, all types of developers need to bear in mind the importance of obtaining accurate site information and to ensure that careful records are maintained of all works undertaken on the site. The ability to communicate this information in ways that are truthful and not misleading is of paramount importance to the success of the project.

This report has been produced at a very important time for the redevelopment of 'previously used' land. When it went to press in July 2000, little over a year had elapsed since the NHBC introduced its new Standards Chapter 4.1 "Land Quality-managing ground conditions" (National House-Building Council 1999) requiring the investigation of all housing sites, greenfield or brownfield, and the extension of the Buildmark Warranty to include contamination. It is understood that initial responses, from developers and consumers, have been favourable.

More recently, in March 2000, the DETR published Planning Policy Guidance Note 3 (PPG3) *Housing*, which introduces the concept of 'sequential testing' to the allocation of housing land for residential development. This requires local authorities to consider the suitability of 'previously used' land before allocating greenfield land for development. In April 2000, the long awaited 'contaminated land legislation', Part IIA of the Environmental Protection Act 1990, came into effect in England only. We are told that the DETR - Environment Agency Contaminated Land Exposure Assessment (CLEA) guidance is 'with the printers' and understand that a new Planning Policy Guidance Note, dealing specifically with contamination and planning, has been drafted and is likely to be sent out for consultation within the next month or two.

All of these are likely to impact the redevelopment process over coming months and years. None of the development examples in this report have adopted innovative or 'new technology' remedial methods, this is perhaps indicative of the wariness felt by the housing development industry and a lack of willingness to take financial risks. In five years time, or even less, developers and their advisors may look at these examples and say "we would not do it that way today". In the meantime, if this report can encourage developers to a greater willingness to tackle the redevelopment of contaminated land and help to bring about an improvement in communications, then it will have achieved its objective.

2. Why use previously used land for new homes?

Many references have been made to '4.4 million new homes by 2016' and '60% of new housing to be constructed on previously used land'[1]. All too often these figures have been misquoted, or used out of context (for example Simpkins, 1997, and Kelly, 1999). The 4.4 million figure related to the creation of new households over a 25 year period from 1991, not to construction targets for new housing. The 60% figure was an overall 'aspirational' target for England, not a requirement for all local authority areas to locate new housing on 'brownfield' land.

The projected increase in household growth was estimated from a number of different statistics - people leaving home an at earlier age, higher divorce rates, people marrying later and living longer, and a limited amount of inward migration. More recent projections in 1996 showed a reduced expectation of household formation, at 3.8 million over 25 years, albeit advanced by five years from the previous projection. Although this is a reduction in projected numbers, it still forms an increase of approximately 19% on the number of households in England at the start of the period (1996)[2].

The 60% figure for turning previously used land into housing sites was already being achieved, or even exceeded, at the time of the 1996 green paper - notably in London and Merseyside - but in some parts of the country there was by no means enough 'brown' land for this target to be achieved. Anyway, it has been argued (see Perowne, 1998) that too much emphasis was being placed on re-using land for housing, when it should be reserved for new industrial and commercial uses.

Land for housing development

The Urban Task Force, chaired by Lord Rogers of Riverside, addressed the problem of delivering land for housing. The Task Force considered that "an accurate assessment of the supply of previously used land is vital, both in terms of ensuring we are maximising the re-use of land and in evaluating the feasibility of the 60% recycling target" (Urban Task Force, 1999, p179).

Using data from a variety of sources, such as the National Land Use Database (NLUD), the DETR Derelict Land Survey (DLS) and the Vacant Land Survey (VLS), the Task Force prepared an assessment. Classifying previously used land as either Derelict or Vacant, the Task Force estimated that the available supply was 28,800 hectares and 16,200 hectares respectively. Of this land, the areas considered to be suitable for housing

---

[1] *Government Green Paper Household Growth: where shall we live? November 1996, HMSO.*
[2] *DETR Press Release 29th March 1999 - www.press.detr.gov.uk*

use were estimated as - Derelict Land 5,600 hectares and Vacant Land 5,300 hectares, in other words 24% of the available stock of Derelict and Vacant land.

The Urban Task Force calculated that these 10,900 hectares could accommodate around 314,000 housing units, using a density of 29 units per hectare (fewer than 12 units per acre) (Urban Task Force, 1999, p179). Given that much of the previously used land deemed suitable for housing development is in urban areas, this estimated number of housing units is probably on the low side. The Task Force considered the issue of higher densities for urban housing and made the following recommendation:

revise planning and funding guidance to:

- **discourage local authorities from using 'density' and 'over-development' as reasons for refusing planning permission;**

- **create a planning presumption against excessively low density urban development;**

- **provide advice on use of density standards linked to design quality."**

(Urban Task Force, 1999, p64)

Adoption of the Task Force's recommendation could not be expected to have an overnight dramatic impact by, say, doubling the density of urban development. It could, however, over the period of the current housing projections, have the effect of increasing the development potential of land identified as suitable for housing use by a further 20-25%, an additional 60,000 to 80,000 housing units.

The Task Force also commented "there is evidence that certain types of derelict land have been under-reported in NLUD", although these were mainly sites felt to be less suitable for redevelopment and that "the VLS only covers vacant urban land, and will not include sites that fall within rural areas." (Urban Task Force, 1999, p178). Increased densities in urban areas and the under-estimation of land supply, including rural 'brownfields', mean therefore that probably between 400,000 and 500,000 new housing units could be accommodated on the 'currently available' stock of previously used land.

In addition to the re-use of derelict and vacant land, the Urban Task Force concluded that currently vacant buildings, e.g. offices, warehouses, retail premises etc., could be converted to provide a further 247,000 housing units. This estimate was based on a number of data sources - NLUD, English Housing Survey and Land Use Change Statistics - and was considered likely to be an underestimate. Taking all of these estimates together, it is likely that something in excess of 750,000 housing units could be provided on currently available, but previously used, land and by converting redundant, structurally sound, unoccupied buildings.

This amount of development potential clearly represents an important resource but still falls a long way short of government aspirations of locating 60% of new housing on previously used land. The Task Force addressed this issue and produced an estimate of projected supply from all sources, including vacant and derelict land, redevelopment of existing uses and urban infilling. The estimate resulted in a projected further 2,087,000 housing units for the period 1996-2021, based on NLUD, academic and consultancy studies, urban capacity studies and the work of the Regional Planning Bodies.

Much of this additional provision, in terms of redevelopable land, is likely to take the form of windfall sites, i.e. sites that were in industrial or commercial use at the time of the most recent Unitary Development Plan (UDP) or Structure Plan, and for which no change of use was envisaged. Landowners may seek to maximise the development potential for such land, by applying for 'higher value' uses, such as retailing or residential, rather than keeping the land for industrial or commercial use. Redevelopment may also bring incompatibilities with other remaining industrial activities in the area. All of which creates problems for local authorities in ensuring an adequate supply of housing development land, especially against policies of 'predict and provide'.

It also presents housing developers with a variety of problems, which may be most apparent in times of house price inflation and in areas of limited land supply. In such situations housing developers are likely to be forced into situations of having to make decisions relating to site acquisitions and form of development whilst not being in full possession of the facts relating to the site.

Some problems associated with the redevelopment of brownfield land

By no means all previously used land is affected by contamination but, when dealing with land which has been in industrial use, the likelihood is that contamination issues will have to be addressed, if only to satisfy the regulators that no contamination exists on the site.

That does not mean that all sites where contamination is found will be so seriously affected as to fall within the scope of the 'contaminated land' legislation in Part IIA of the Environmental Protection Act 1990[3]. This legislation came into effect in England on 1st April 2000 and is designed to tackle the problems associated with the most seriously contaminated land, where significant harm is being (or is likely to be) caused to human health or the environment.

The legislation, and the regulations which bring it into effect, is extremely complex, involving a series of tests to determine whether the land falls within the scope of the legislation and who should be responsible for meeting the cost of remediation. Further details on the legislation and in particular the 'Exclusion Tests' is contained in Appendix 1.

---

[3] *Introduced through section 57 of the Environment 1995.*

The legislation is as yet untested and it is not yet known how keen the regulators (the local authorities and the Environment Agency) are going to be in pursuing its enforcement. Prudent developers will therefore need to ascertain whether or not the local authorities have any plans to take enforcement action in respect of potential development sites, which may result in them being designated as contaminated.

The local authorities also have an essential role to play, as planning authorities, in the redevelopment process, especially as many 'previously used' sites will not have been allocated for housing use in the UDP or the Structure Plan. Many of the developers and consultants interviewed as part of the previous study (Syms, 1997) were very critical of local planning authorities in the context of reusing contaminated land, with much of the blame being attributed to poor communications between planning and environmental health departments. Town planning and other regulatory aspects of redevelopment form part of a parallel study, looking at the re-use of brownfield land in a much wider context than housing (Syms, 2000). It was clear from the case studies research that by no means all town planning authorities place obstacles in front of redevelopment proposals.

Nevertheless, it should be recognised that, in spite of Government policies, legislation and the desires of local authorities to see land re-used, the process of redevelopment is by no means straightforward. Dennis Brant, Chief Executive of George Wimpey PLC, has firmly held views that regulations are impeding the industry, and commented **"It's just as tortuous to get planning permission on a brownfield as it is on a greenfield."** (Ashton, 2000).

The Urban Task Force assessed that 10,900 hectares of derelict and vacant land were suitable for housing development but that does not mean that it is 'developable', or that planning permission will be forthcoming. The planning authority may be reluctant to lose 'employment land' and thus be opposed to residential use, or it may require a comprehensive site investigation before it is even prepared to consider the planning application. Fighting the opposition to residential development and undertaking a full site investigation during the inception phase of the development both take time and money, as a result potential developers may be deterred in their efforts to redevelop previously used land.

Contamination and planning problems are only two of the issues that the intending developer may have to face in returning land to use. Site access is an important consideration, for without adequate access the previously used site is unlikely to be developable even though it is possible to resolve physical ground condition problems. One case study site, in Salford, was contaminated, and contained major underground obstructions. For the intending developer, however, these problems paled into insignificance when compared to the available, somewhat tortuous, access through congested streets of terraced housing and the constraints imposed by the local authority's planning brief.

Related to access problems are issues such as the closure of existing streets, or the diversion of public footpaths, so as to ensure comprehensive redevelopment. One relatively small development, on a site of less than two hectares, required two street closure orders and one footpath diversion - the latter being challenged by an organisation more normally associated with protecting ramblers rights of way through fells and dales than inner cities (Syms, 1995). The same small site also required the acquisition of 19 interests in the land.

Even when land owners and occupiers are prepared to sell by agreement, site assembly may still be fraught with problems. In many industrial towns and cities the freehold interest in 19th Century housing developments was retained by the original developers or factory owners, who granted subsidiary interests for terms of 99 or even 999 years. Whilst it may be possible to purchase these leasehold interests and even compensate occupational tenants, identifying the owner of the freehold interest may be impossible. The developer may therefore be faced with either a lengthy legal process or creating modern sub-leases, for terms of say 750 or 800 years and selling these in lieu of freeholds.

Third party rights and easements can seriously impede the developer's progress and need to be taken into account early in the planning/legal process. Such rights are not always apparent from the documentation but may also be implied. The grant of planning permission gives no comfort that 'third party' rights can be overridden. For example, rights to light acquired by prescription i.e. a minimum of 20 years of enjoyment, are a particular thorn in the developers side. In such cases specialist surveying advice may be necessary and the only solution an expensive compromise with an adjoining owner.

Party Wall issues are generally easier to resolve in practice following the Party Wall Act 1996. However, issues can arise which were unforeseen by the legislation, e.g. what happens when a building owner changes in the course of a Party Wall Award?

The provision of services, drainage, water, electricity, gas and telecommunications, is essential for all new developments and, at first sight, may not appear to be a major issue for previously used land. One might assume, for example, that the former uses had mains services connected, or at least drainage, water, electricity and telephone.

This may be the case but the drainage system may be an old combined sewer, of insufficient capacity for the new development. Similarly the water supply that previously served a factory employing several hundred people may be totally inadequate for twenty or thirty houses. Electricity and telephone capacities, which previously served the industrial user may have been re-allocated elsewhere by the service provider following closure of the plant. This may result in the need for extensive off-site infrastructure works before supplies can be provided to the new development.

Existing services and the provision of new services may also present problems in terms of site contamination, as service trenches and ducts are likely to provide preferential pathways for the migration of contaminants.

One issue largely outside the control of the intending developer is the potential impact on the development caused by 'bad neighbour' type adjoining land uses. Unsightly, noisy and odorous activities may well render an area unacceptable for housing development. It may be possible to counter the effects of 'unsightliness' by ensuring that the residential development creates its own self-contained environment and to design against noise through the careful siting of windows and the use of double, or even triple, glazing. In more extreme situations, especially where obnoxious odours are concerned, the developer may be faced with little choice but to abandon the project or to redevelop the land for some non-residential purpose, that is unless the local authority is prepared to take action to relocate the offending activity.

Although the principal focus of the case studies in the following chapters is the resolution of land contamination issues, these other barriers to redevelopment will be addressed where the developers concerned have encountered them.

So why re-use land for housing?

With the variety of problems described above, any developer could be forgiven for deciding only to construct housing on 'greenfield' land. Admittedly the issues to be taken into account are frequently complex but developers are unlikely to be successful if they adopt a negative attitude towards the re-use of land. In many cities and larger industrial towns the demand for new housing simply cannot be accommodated on greenfield sites.

Government housing policy is clearly in favour of re-using brownfield land for housing, as set out in the 1996 green paper and, more recently, confirmed in the revised Planning Policy Guidance note 3 *Housing* (DETR, 2000). A brief outline of PPG3 is contained in Appendix 2 but, in the context of re-using land, one very important aspect is the introduction of a 'sequential test' whereby town planners are required to consider the suitability of 'previously-developed' land when allocating land for residential development in local plans and Unitary Development Plans.

One important answer to this question, which is often overlooked, is that many brownfield sites are in good locations, where there is either a housing need or where people want to live. Good access to places of employment, by foot or public transport, shopping and leisure facilities all serve to strengthen the argument in favour of re-using land.

3. Technical problems and solutions for the redevelopment of brownfield land

Introduction

The redevelopment of brownfield land will present any developer with a number of technical and non-technical problems. These problems, which are discussed in greater detail below, will have repercussions in terms of a development's design and cost. When considering a brownfield site a developer will need to satisfy regulators that any finished development will not pose any unacceptable risk to the eventual occupiers, and to be satisfied that the proposed scheme can be delivered inside any set financial targets.

Identifying potential problems caused by land contamination

Prior to purchasing a site (greenfield or brownfield) a developer should employ a suitably qualified consultant to undertake a preliminary assessment of the subject site in order to identify any possible hazards that may affect future development. This assessment should include a desk study and a walkover survey (see Department of the Environment Contaminated Land Research Reports CLR2 and CLR3, amongst others). A desk study will involve the collection and analysis of all available data and a walkover survey will involve a direct inspection of the site and surrounding area using information from the desk study. Box 3.1 shows the sources and types of information available to consultants when undertaking the desk study.

Assembly of the information available from the sources in Box 3.1 should provide an understanding of the various stages of development that have taken place on site. The walkover survey allows the consultant to check information obtained from the desk study and may add further detail.

'A visual assessment of the site may disclose evidence of unrecorded events and activities, particularly those which post-date available records, e.g. fly-tipping' (Welsh Development Agency, 1993, p.3.4).

Box 3.1 Sources and types of information

Source	Materials
Local Library	Maps, current and historic, books, journals, trade directories, newspaper records and magazine articles.
Ordnance Survey	Large scale current and superseded maps
National map libraries	Various maps
British Geological Survey, universities, and local bodies, e.g. Greater Manchester Geological Unit	Geological maps and memoirs, well and exploration records, hydrogeological records
Coal Authority	Coal mining records
Minerals Planning Authority	Mineral extraction records
Public utilities	Location of services
Local authorities	Town planning registers and enforcement notices. Environmental health consents and enforcement or abatement notices
Present and previous owners, occupier and users	Details of activities and processes carried and users out. Plans and photographs
Environment Agency and water undertakings	Surface water run-off, outfall details Licensed waste disposal activities, sludge spreading. River and canal details, eg water quality and abstraction licensing
Drainage authorities	Surface water drainage and improvement schemes
Aerial photographic libraries	Historical and modern photography
Local museums and County archaeologists	Maps, industrial histories, photographs and artefacts
English Heritage	Historical aerial photographs
Goad maps and insurance information	Maps and other records relating to use of buildings

Sources: Department of the Environment Contaminated Land Research Report 3 and Syms 1999, p2

Figure 3.1 Contaminant-pathway-receptor - significant pollutant linkages

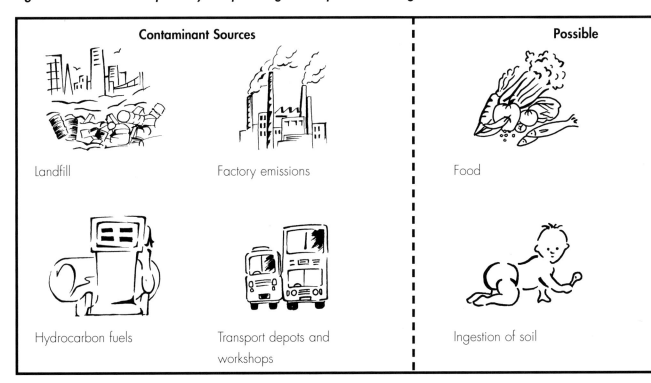

The desk study and the walkover survey will allow the consultant to characterise the site and assess its suitability for housing development. In terms of land contamination the consultant will characterise the site in relation to its potential to cause harm or pollution of controlled waters. This is assessed using a **contaminant-pathway-receptor** risk model, where the contaminant (or source) relates to a substance or group of substances with the potential to cause harm, the receptor (sometimes referred to as the target) is someone or something that could be harmed by the contaminant and the pathway is the route through which it could reach the receptor. The contaminant-pathway-receptor approach is the same as that used by regulatory authorities for assessing the potential to cause 'significant harm' on a site that is potentially contaminated in the legal sense. For each contaminant and possible receptor the regulatory authority has to determine whether or not a 'significant pollutant linkage' exists.

The site investigation

The site investigation should be undertaken on a phased basis, proceeding from a preliminary site assessment to a comprehensive understanding of the soil conditions. In this way the earlier work can be used to determine the nature of the subsequent phases and thus facilitate development of a conceptual model.

The preliminary site assessment will identify parts of the site where there may be the possibility of contamination and highlight areas for further investigation. The brief to the consultants and their terms of appointment should provide for the possibility of the

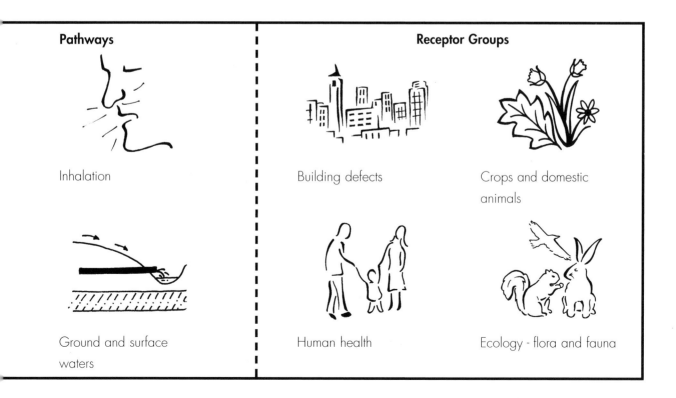

Pathways	Receptor Groups	
Inhalation	Building defects	Crops and domestic animals
Ground and surface waters	Human health	Ecology - flora and fauna

investigation being terminated following submission of the preliminary report. This is in case the degree of contamination identified is beyond that which the developer is prepared to consider and the decision is taken not to continue with the project (Syms, 1997, p77).

It should be stressed that no ground investigation can guarantee to locate all contaminants that may exist within a site and be able to quantify their extent and volume. The objective of an investigation should be to assess, with a reasonable degree of certainty, the likelihood of any contamination being present, the nature of the contaminants themselves and the media in which they are located.

The main site investigation will involve taking a number of samples, solid and liquid (where appropriate), from different parts of the site and at regular depths. The preliminary site assessment can be used in order to undertake a cost effective intrusive site investigation. It should enable the location of possible contaminants to be determined with a reasonable degree of accuracy. Sampling therefore may be concentrated around possible 'hot-spots' with the possibility of less intensive sampling over other areas of the site.

The environmental consultant employed should, at least, follow the advice given in Contaminated Land Research Report CLR 4, *Sampling Strategies for Contaminated Land* (Department of the Environment, 1994b), or Volume III *Site investigation and assessment* of the CIRIA 'Remedial Treatment for Contaminated Land' series, as to the minimum number of sampling points required. Further guidance will be contained in CIRIA 599, due to be published in Autumn 2000. The Association of Geotechnical and Geoenvironmental Specialists (AGS) has also produced guidelines for good practice in site investigation - www.ags.org.uk.

The information thus obtained from the site investigation can then be used in selecting the appropriate method, or methods, of treatment and designing the programme of remediation.

Collecting samples

The samples will usually be collected using trial pits or boreholes. For most forms of shallow contamination, a trial pit investigation is likely to be most appropriate, as this method facilitates visual inspection of both the contaminants and the media within which they are contained. For volatile contaminants, however, trial pits and trench methods are inappropriate due to the problem of sample collection, and a borehole investigation will produce better results. (Syms, 1997, p84). In situations where there is the possibility of escaping gas or liquids a number of temporary or permanent 'probes' can be used. These are especially useful in areas of the site which cannot easily be accessed by other site machinery.

The ground investigation should be designed in such a way as to characterise the contamination present within the site with respect to:

- lateral and vertical extent

- chemical composition and concentration

- physical characteristics (e.g. volatility, solubility)

- biological characteristics (e.g. pathenogenicity, degradation potential)

(Source: Welsh Development Agency, 1993, pp 3.11-3.12)

Site investigators must ensure that appropriate sampling techniques are used, in order to avoid cross contamination, and that samples are properly handled and stored, so that they do not deteriorate prior to arrival at the laboratory. Following the intrusive site investigation samples will be sent for analysis at an appropriate laboratory (e.g. UKAS accredited) and 'chain of custody' records must be maintained in respect of all samples. Not all samples will need to be tested for a full suite of contaminants, as this is usually both unnecessary and costly. Instead, a site specific testing regime should be developed. The contaminants to be tested for should be determined by reference to the nature of the former activities on the site, the raw materials used and the products/wastes produced.

Where housing is the proposed end use, the results of the chemical analysis have, in the past, usually been measured in relation to ICRCL[4] criteria for domestic gardens, or in some cases by reference to Dutch Intervention Values which have no legal standing in the United Kingdom. The guidance has been used as a way of setting acceptable remediation criteria for housing development but the design of a scheme may allow for some less contaminated material to remain on site, e.g. under roads and driveways. It should however be stressed that the ICRCL list refers to only 20 contaminants, yet some of the DETR Industry Profiles list more than 100 possible contaminants from industrial uses (Sherritt, 2000). The site investigator should base the laboratory testing regime on the historical nature of activities on the site.

The new Contaminated Land Exposure Assessment (CLEA) Guidance Values produced for the Department of Environment, Transport and the Regions should enable a more appropriate, site specific, assessment to be made. The CLEA Guidance Values are based on toxicology data and are expected to be published during 2000. Table 3.1 contains suggested threshold and action levels for some commonly found contaminants, by reference to ICRCL and Dutch guidance. As this report went to press, publication of the Environment Agency's "Guidance for the Safe Development of Housing on Land affected by Contamination" was understood to be imminent (Baker, 2000), this will provide further guidance.

[4] *The Interdepartmental Committee for the Redevelopment of Contaminated Land.*

Table 3.1 Indicative threshold and action levels for some common contaminants

Contaminant	Housing with domestic gardens/play areas	Housing with communal gardens	Other buildings & hard cover (roads etc)	Landscaped areas/parks
METALS Cadmium mg/kg Chromium -Total mg/kg -Hexavalent mg/kg Lead mg/kg Mercury mg/kg	ICRCL THRESHOLD 3 600 25 500 1	ICRCL THRESHOLD 3 600 25 500 1	ICRCL THRESHOLD 15 1,000 25 500 20	ICRCL THRESHOLD 15 1,000 25 500 20
Arsenic mg/kg	10	10	40	40
Cyanide (Free) mg/kg Cyanide (Complex) mg/kg	25 250	25 250	100 250	100 250
Phytotoxic Metals Copper, Nickel, Zinc mg/kg	1,000 (sum of all 3)	1,000 (sum of all 3)	1,000 (sum of all 3)	1,000 (sum of all 3)
Polycyclic Aromatic Hydrocarbons mg/kg	ICRCL THRESHOLD 50	ICRCL ACTION 500	ICRCL ACTION 10,000	ICRCL ACTION 10,000
Phenols mg/kg	5	200	1,000	1,000
Sulphate	2,000 mg/kg	10,000 mg/kg	Ref. to BRE Digest 363	10,000 mg/kg
Mineral oil mg/kg	DUTCH TARGET 50	DUTCH INTERVENTION 5,000	DUTCH INTERVENTION 5,000	DUTCH INTERVENTION 5,000
Gasoline (Volatile Organic Compunds) PID measurement	1/4 occupational exposure limit for benzene (ppm) 1.2 ppm	1/4 occupational exposure limit for benzene (ppm) 1.2 ppm	1/4 occupational exposure limit for benzene (ppm) 1.2 ppm	Occupational exposure limit for benzene (ppm) 5 ppm
Polychlorinated Biphenyls mg/kg	DUTCH TARGET 0.02	DUTCH TARGET 0.02	DUTCH INTERVENTION 1	DUTCH INTERVENTION 1
Toluene Extractable Matter mg/kg	2,000	2,000	2,000	2,000
Total Petroleum Hydrocarbons (TPH's) mg/kg	100	100	100	1,000

Source: Acer, 1995 report

No two sites are identical and site specific assessments may enable the retention on site of soil containing contaminants at significantly higher concentrations than those listed in Table 3.1. This may be achieved by, for example, using moderately contaminated spoilt to form earth mounding and landscaping areas or to fill voids under hard surfaces.

The Investigation Report

The results of the site investigation will be presented in a detailed report, which should provide a step-by-step account of works undertaken. The report should be of a non-technical nature in order that the developer and appropriate regulatory authorities may understand it. It will include information relating to the site history, sampling strategy, analysis of results, maps showing trial-pit and bore-hole locations, site profiles, remediation strategies and a set of summary conclusions.

If the original site investigation identified contamination of a nature that was unexpected from the historical study, then a supplementary site investigation may be recommended. Such a discovery of unexpected contaminants may, in some cases, lead to a developer withdrawing interest from a site. The developer may well have incurred a substantial abortive cost but, in general, an under-designed site investigation has the potential to result in even higher unexpected costs during the development period and an increase in the timescale of the project, both of which will affect its profitability.

It should be noted that the use of reports might be limited by confidentiality clauses, professional liability and non-disclosure agreements. Therefore it may not be possible for a developer to rely upon a report prepared for a land owner, or a third party, and enquiries will have to be made to determine whether or not the consultant who prepared the report is prepared to enter into a collateral warranty, or to give duty of care to a new owner. Even if the consultant is prepared to warrant the report, the prospective developer should exercise extreme caution, especially if the investigation was not recent, as site conditions may have changed since the report was prepared.

Remediation options

Various options exist for the remediation of different types of contamination. These include:

- **Excavation and disposal**

- **Containment (in-situ or ex-situ)**

- **Soil Treatment Methods**

Excavation and disposal

This simply involves the excavation of contaminated material and removal to a licensed landfill site. 1.5M tonnes of contaminated material is disposed of this way each year in the UK (POST, 1998, p.28). At the present time this is the favoured option for many developers as it is not an excessively technical solution, is relatively quick and is generally cheaper than other options available. Banks and other financial institutions have, historically, favoured the excavation and disposal approach as it deals with the contamination problem once and for all. This research report shows that this situation is beginning to change, with developers and their funders looking to other options as suitably licensed tips become scarcer and more expensive. At the present time it is possible for developers to obtain exemption from the payment of Landfill Tax in situations where it is necessary to remove contaminants for off-site disposal. Anecdotal evidence suggests, however, that by no means all developers are seeking exemption and are simply factoring in the Landfill Tax as a development cost. This may be because the exemption is not guaranteed and takes time to obtain.

Containment

This can either involve contaminants being isolated from the site user and the wider environment where they lie (in-situ), or where they have been moved to within specially constructed landfills on the site (ex-situ). (POST, 1998, 28). Techniques for containment include:

- building 'walls' of impermeable clay (e.g. bentonite) around and possibly under the contaminated material;

- capping the area with coarse material to prevent movement of contaminants by capillary action;

- creating an impermeable layer using clay or a plastic 'geo-textile' liner.

Monitoring may be required for a period of time, due to the fact that contaminants are not removed from the site. Care should also be taken when using such systems to ensure that groundwater moving through the site cannot 'flush-out' any contaminants, and to vent methane and carbon dioxide emitted from the decay of organic materials in the soil by micro-organisms. (POST, 1998, 28)

In terms of the final development the ex-situ method is likely to be inappropriate for housing development, in most cases, as a Waste Management Licence may be required and purchasers could become apprehensive when solicitors searches reveal that there is a waste management facility on site. For some forms of treatment, for example, bio-remediation or low temperature thermal desorption, it may be possible to obtain a Mobile Plant Licence, for machinery brought onto the site to carry out the treatment work and which will then be removed once the work has been completed. This should overcome any 'stigma' that might attach to a site, compared to the alternative of post-development monitoring being carried out under a Waste Management Licence.

Soil treatment methods

There are a number of soil treatment methods, some of which have been used successfully where housing was the proposed end-use and others are at the present time still in their experimental stages. These methods include:

Physical treatment technologies

Physical treatments can be used to separate soil contaminants and include:

- **Soil washing** - separating soil into 'clean' and 'dirty' fractions according to their relative affinities for different types of soil particle. The soils are washed with water, detergents, acids, alkalis or solvents. The objective being to reduce the volume of contaminated material and the clean fraction can be returned to the site. The contaminated residue, in which the contaminants are more concentrated than previously, is disposed of to landfill or subjected to further treatment. The washing water is recycled within the plant.

- **Vapour Extraction** - 'sucking' air through the soil (via a network of wells and pipes) to remove volatile contaminants (e.g. petrol), which can be treated (e.g. by passing through activated carbon filters or catalytic oxidisers) before the air is released into the atmosphere.

Biological treatment technologies

Bio-remediation relies on the ability of soil micro-organisms (e.g. bacteria and fungi) to break down contaminants naturally. This can be accelerated and optimised by altering the conditions for the micro-organisms (e.g. altering the supply of oxygen, water and nutrients). There has also been some recent work into using specialist or genetically modified plants to extract contaminants from the soil. Biological techniques include:

- **Landfarming** - based on agricultural practice, with the contaminated soil being spread over the surface to a thickness of around 0.5m, being regularly mixed to improve soil structure and oxygen supply;

- **Windrow turning** - similar to landfarming but with the soil in thicker layers and materials such as woodchips or compost introduced to improve soil structure;

- **Engineered soil banks or 'biopiles'** - where the soil is placed in a static heap, nutrients are added and biological processes are stimulated through aeration and water supply;

- **Slurry-phase biodegradation** - where pre-treated soils are slurried with water and treated in a reactor with a mechanical agitation device;

- **Bioventing** - an in-situ process through which the natural biodegradation process is optimised through the addition of nutrients and oxygen to the soil.

- **Phyto-remediation** - using plants to take-up the contaminants from the soil, e.g. willow coppicing.

Of the currently available treatment technologies, physical and biological treatments are most likely to be employed in preparing land for residential development. Other treatments include chemical treatments, thermal technologies which may be considered to be environmentally unacceptable in some locations, and solidification and stabilisation treatments. They are generally expensive and untried in the UK.

Chemical treatment technologies

These involve converting contaminants into alternative chemical forms to either destroy them or render them less environmentally harmful, for example, liming to increase the pH.

Thermal treatment technologies

These include **thermal stripping**, heating the soil to drive off any volatile contaminants for collection and disposal, and **incineration**, the high temperature burning of contaminants in the soil to destroy most organic contaminants.

Solidification and stabilisation technologies

Solidification and **stabilisation** includes mixing contaminated soil with a binder material such as asphalt and cement to produce a stable and inert product. This technique effectively immobilises heavy metals, but other contaminants may be leached out by ground water. Vitrification is the conversion of the soil into glass through a high temperature process to immobilise the contaminants in beads or blocks.

The above summary provides only the briefest information regarding available treatment technologies and there are many variations of the different technologies, including proprietary methodologies. For a more comprehensive review readers are referred to *A Review of Full Scale Treatment Technologies for the Remediation of Contaminated Soil* by Ian Martin and Paul Bardos (1996), which is the final report of a study undertaken for the Royal Commission on Environmental Pollution.

Choice of treatment method

The selection of the most appropriate options will often have a significant impact on the viability of a housing development. The choice of remediation method may be influenced by a number of factors:

• cost of the works relative to site value or end value of the proposed development;

• neighbouring land uses;

• the nature of the proposed housing development, for example, different methods may be adopted on a site to be developed with 'starter' homes for young families, with individual gardens, compared to sheltered housing for the elderly with communal gardens;

• legal & regulatory issues, including implications under Part IIA of the Environmental Protection Act 1990, the 'contaminated land legislation';

• surrounding environment, which may rule out some options due to environmental or social constraints;

- geography, geology and hydrogeology, which may limit the range of solutions;

- time-scale, for example meeting market demands or compliance with planning/regulatory requirements;

- technical limitations of the treatment processes, evaluation and agreement as to any residual risks.

The treatment method, or methods, will need to be approved by the appropriate regulatory authorities. This will involve getting the approval of Planners, Environmental Health Officer, Building Control Officers, Environment Agency Officers and the NHBC or other insurers. Developers should also consider the implications of Part IIA of the Environmental Protection Act 1990 where contaminants are to be left on site to ensure that pollution is not caused to controlled waters at a future date. All approvals must be properly documented if future repercussions and possible stigmatisation of the development are to be avoided. It is most inadvisable to commence work on the site remediation before all necessary approvals have been obtained and could be a costly mistake.

Development of sites in built-up areas may preclude the use of treatment methods that involve large production of dust, noise and/or odours. The site layout and topography may preclude the use of certain specialist machines. There may also be other constraints which limit the choice of remedial methods.

The time scales involved in developing many sites mean that for the individual housing developer the only economical options are excavation and removal or containment, or a mixture of both. Good neighbour relations can pay dividends and assist the redevelopment process. In many instances the developer will be the party undertaking the remediation, however, there are a number of examples of large parcels of land, for example owned by British Gas, which have been remediated economically using more innovative soil treatment methods and subsequently sold to housing developers.

Whichever treatment method is adopted in the final development the developer needs to be certain that any unacceptable risks are removed or are properly addressed and that all works carried out are clearly documented and recorded for future reference. This includes the contractor keeping a detailed site diary of the remedial works, all vehicles movements onto and off the site (removing contaminated spoil and importing clean fill) and all Waste Transfer notes. It is as important to keep records of imported fill material, including laboratory test results, as it is to record details of materials disposed of to landfill.

All works, whether they involve excavation and disposal, containment or soil treatment, must be supervised by suitably experienced professionals, validated and warranted. Should regulators or purchasers later require information relating to remedial works it can then be provided. Most importantly, should the information be required as part of the property transfer process, whether on first sale or subsequent sales, it should be readily available and in a form that is easily assimilated.

KEY POINTS

- Whenever undertaking a housing development (greenfield or brownfield) it is essential to undertake a preliminary site assessment.

- Employ a suitably qualified environmental consultant to undertake the preliminary site assessment and site investigation, agree a brief, fee and costs.

- Use the preliminary site assessment to identify possible 'hot-spots' and design a sampling strategy.

- Undertake a phased site investigation.

- Identify the most cost effective technique for removing unacceptable risks from site - the easiest method might not necessarily be the cheapest or most suitable.

- Prepare a completion report, including validation of the work undertaken in compliance with the remediation strategy, so that regulators and purchasers can be provided with relevant information should it be needed at a later date.

4. Brickworks, shallow mine workings, road haulage, made ground

- EXCAVATION AND OFF-SITE DISPOSAL/ENCAPSULATION/RECYCLING OF ASH
- PRIVATE FOR SALE

Location:	Oughtibridge, Sheffield.
Size of site:	3.24 hectares
Contaminants:	heavy metals and hydrocarbons
Potential receptors:	building workers, occupiers

This is a development of 81 three and four bedroom detached houses by Redrow and Bryant Homes. The site is situated to the north-west of Sheffield and was most recently used as a road haulage yard. Previously it had been a brickworks, see the 1934 map extract Figure 4.1, and the subject of extensive shallow mining. Further development occurred between 1934 and 1958 with the addition of a number of buildings towards Station Lane.

The site forms a long tongue of levelled made ground, having been filled over several years with ash and clinker. This resulted in approximately 10m of fill in some areas of the site. A railway line forms the eastern boundary and a steep slope (1:2) forms the western boundary down to the River Don in the valley. The northern part of the site adjoins Oughtibridge Lane and the southern edge is bounded by woodland.

The site had been identified in the Sheffield UDP for industrial purposes. It had also been considered as a car park should the railway line be opened for public transport. The haulage company (the owner) was seeking to sell the site and move to premises nearer the motorway network. Sheffield City Council was aware that there was a high demand for housing in this area and, because the subject site was surrounded by existing housing, the Council was willing to accept a change of use. All the houses were for sale and there was no social housing on the site. The developer entered into a S.106 agreement of the Town & Country Planning Act 1990 to provide eight houses which met current mobility standards and provide a sum of money to improve a nearby park. The developer also had to provide some traffic calming measures.

Due to the possibility of the site being contaminated the planning authority required a full geotechnical and contamination survey to be undertaken. The site investigation and remediation was designed and supervised by AIG Consultants, under a fixed price contract. This was the preferred option of the developer so that additional costs would not be incurred at a later date.

The site investigation was carried out in phases using a mix of boreholes and trial pits. These were used to determine the nature and depth of the fill material as well as trying to target possible hot-spots of concern. In excess of 100 samples were taken, of which 40 were analysed.

The site investigation revealed that ash and clinker were present across the whole site. The minimum thickness was 7 metres to a maximum of 10 metres. The investigation revealed unacceptable levels of arsenic, zinc, copper, nickel and cadmium, contained in the fill material across the whole site. Localised areas of organic contamination, fuel oils from spillages and contamination from leaking underground storage tanks were found. These contaminants all related to the previous use as a haulage yard.

There was little contamination with respect to the brickworks other than the ash and clinker. Gas monitoring samples revealed no methane although there were slightly elevated amounts of carbon dioxide. The geotechnical survey revealed that the made ground was not in a very good state of consolidation. The leachability tests revealed that there were no mobile contaminants and that there was no threat to groundwater.

Various options were considered for remediation of the site. Bio-remediation could have been used to deal with the organic contamination but it was considered that the volume of material would have been too small to deal with cost effectively. Therefore the organic contaminated material was excavated and removed to a licensed landfill.

The ash and clinker could not practically be removed to licensed landfill due to the large volumes involved. As the site investigation had revealed that the metal contaminants in the ash and clinker were not leachable and did not represent a risk to controlled waters a cover system was deemed to be the most appropriate solution. This enables the pathway to be broken between the contaminants and potential receptors - the house occupiers and building workers.

Recycling was one option considered for the ash, as this material can be reused by building block manufacturers. However, there are only certain grades of material that they will accept. On this development the environmental consultant recognised that some of the ash could be sold in order to make the scheme economically viable. A block manufacturer agreed to take the waste from the site and reclamation began in March 1998. In total approximately 40% of the ash was removed from site. The remaining ash and clinker was compacted to make a suitable foundation stratum.

There were no problems associated with obtaining planning permission, which included a condition that details of the remediation scheme be submitted and agreed prior to commencement of development. Information and data from the site investigations were duly agreed with the regulators. Sheffield City Council's Environmental Health Department was willing to accept the proposed reclamation scheme. They stipulated that during remedial works a wheel wash facility needed to be used and that the off site roads must be kept clean.

There was a slight problem when the Environment Agency questioned the destination of the waste material. The Agency officer felt that the recipient of the waste wasn't a licensed waste repository. The developer argued that it was not a waste but a recycled material and that it did not need to be consigned to a licensed waste repository. Following a series of meetings the developer was allowed to continue with the remediation of the site. In spite of this, the developer's view of the experience with the authorities was very good and it was felt that a good relationship was established between the consultants and regulating officers.

The remedial works were supervised by the environmental consultant and an on-site engineer was employed throughout. The remediation works took approximately six months to complete and, in addition to the ash removed for recycling, a total of 25,000m³ of other material was removed to a licensed landfill. Other site preparation works included grouting former shallow mine workings.

Following removal of the ash layer the site was capped with one metre of clay. This was then covered with inert top soil. The remedial works were delayed by approximately one month, partly due to the problems with the Environment Agency, but also due to limited access and constraints on site. The fact that the two developers were trying to commence work whilst remedial works were still ongoing, provided a further complication. These issues had a subsequent 'knock-on' effect in terms of completing the housing scheme.

Buildings that had occupied the site prior to development were crushed and used as hardcore under the roads. Houses constructed on engineered fill were built on reinforced concrete rafts and other houses were built using conventional strip foundations.

The development is now complete and all the houses occupied. The houses were sold by 'in-house' sales teams and the sales literature had information relating to the former use of the site in order to comply with the Property Mis-descriptions Act 1996. In the transfer documentation there is an extract of the ground investigation that includes an executive summary and a remediation statement.

A post remediation completion report has been provided for the developer that includes all documentation, details of works undertaken, finished levels, details of hot-spots and results of the imported inert material testing. The development and reclamation works have been insured by NHBC. With the benefit of hindsight, the developer felt that it would have been preferable to complete the remediation before commencing the development work and that some of the approval response times could have been improved.

Comment

The remediation in this case study minimised the disposal of contaminated material to a licensed landfill. The sale of ash to the block manufacturer enabled the scheme to be economically viable.

The fixed fee paid to the environmental consultant for undertaking all investigations and remedial works enabled the developer to identify all costs at the outset. However, care does need to be taken when entering into combined consultancy and remediation contracts.

The works have been completed to the satisfaction of the local authority and NHBC, and have been fully documented.

KEY POINTS

- Explore with the local planning authority the possibility of changing the use from industrial to housing.

- Consider obtaining a fixed price quote from the environmental consultant for all investigation and remediation work and, whether under a fixed price or otherwise, agree a brief for the work to be undertaken.

- Examine all remediation options, including reusing any materials on site or the possibility of selling any materials, such as ash, from a site.

- Identify any access or site constraints which may affect development - it may be preferable on some sites to allow all remediation works to be completed before development commences.

DETR Industry Profiles: Road vehicle fuelling, service and repair: transport and haulage centres; Waste recycling: landfills and other waste treatment or waste disposal sites

---

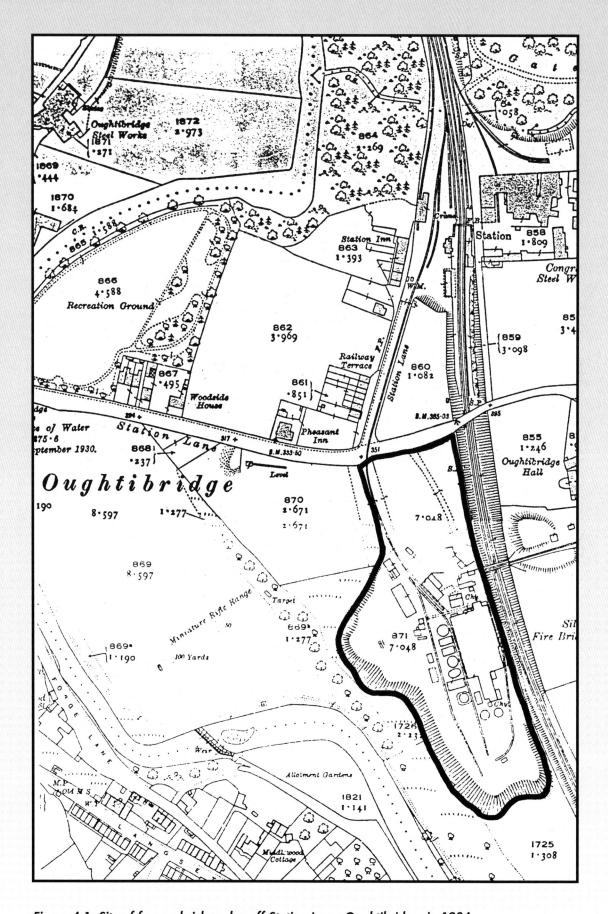

Figure 4.1 Site of former brickworks, off Station Lane, Oughtibridge, in 1934

5. Cotton mill, bleach works, oil seals manufacture

- REMEDIATION METHOD, NOT FINALISED
- PRIVATE HOUSING TO RENT

Location:	**Pendleton, Salford**
Size of site:	**1.75 hectares**
Contaminants:	**heavy metals, hydrocarbons**
Principal receptor:	**ground and surface waters, building workers, occupiers**

This development site is one of three sites in the Charlestown area of Pendleton, for which Salford City Council has prepared a development brief. The site is within the City Council's Pendleton Project, an initiative designed to secure the revitalisation of the area through physical improvements, economic and community development, improvements in education and a commitment to increased standards of maintenance and environmental quality. It is also within the Croal Irwell Valley Initiative, where the Council is encouraging environmental and access improvements. The River Irwell forms the northern boundary. The site was owned by a local company, which manufactured oil seals for the automotive industry. The company relocated to more modern premises within the city, leaving the Pendleton site vacant.

The site is generally surrounded by industrial uses, although there is some terraced housing to the east and a school to the west. It has a long history of industrial use, pre-dating the industrial revolution. After the site had been vacated the buildings were vandalised and became unsafe. All buildings on the site were therefore demolished although there are extensive drains, culverts and gullies remaining below the surface.

Examination of historical maps shows that cotton mills existed on the site in 1840, with a dock from the River Irwell. By 1893 Irwell Bleach Works occupied the site, a use that existed until at least 1933, see site plan, Figure 5.1. In 1953 the use of the site was described as manufacture of oil seals and there was also an electricity sub-station on site. Geological records indicate that the site is in an area of Bunter sandstone overlain by Alluvial clay, sands and gravels.

The design brief states that the City Council would like to see the site developed for housing with a strip of land, of approximately 15 metres in width, retained alongside the river to provide a footpath/cycle route together with landscaping using native species.

A limited site investigation was undertaken in 1994, consisting of several trial pits apparently not exceeding two metres in depth. This was prior to demolition of the buildings. The investigation revealed extensive soil contamination comprising arsenic, cadmium, phenols, lead, chromium and PAHs, together with boron, copper, nickel and zinc, all being in excess of the ICRCL threshold trigger levels for gardens. Fill material existed across most of the site and it was not clear whether this was due to past uses, or imported fill to raise the ground level for flood protection. The report recommended that it would not be feasible or economic to remove all the contamination and that a layer of granular material would be required, topped by at least 1.0 metre of compacted clay, to act as a capillary break.

A further investigation was undertaken in 1997, after demolition, when eighteen trial pits were excavated to a minimum of four metres depth. Analysis of samples indicated elevated readings of arsenic, copper, lead and zinc, together with three areas showing very elevated readings for Solvent Extractable Matter and Volatile Organic Compounds which indicates the presence of hydrocarbon contamination. The areas of extensive hydrocarbon contamination had spread as a plume across the centre of the site at a depth of between 1.5 and 3.4 metres which was in contact with groundwater in the sands and gravel. This investigation classified the site as a high hazard rating, indicating that extensive remediation was required in order to protect workers on site and future occupiers, together with the River Irwell. Whilst the river had a chemical grading of E (poor), efforts were being made to improve the water quality and to protect the wildlife corridor. In view of the potential for leaching of contamination into the river, the report recommended immediate remedial treatment, regardless of whether or not the site was developed for housing use.

In addition to the contamination the investigation found a number of substantial below ground obstructions, including foundations and machine bases that probably pre-dated the most recent industrial activities on the site. At some time in the past, production on the site had been water powered, drawing water from the River Irwell adjacent to a weir. No evidence of this remained on the surface but the associated underground chambers were located during the investigation.

Access to the site was less than adequate for the new development, being through narrow streets of terraced houses. Improvement of the access would have entailed purchase of the industrial property adjacent to the southern boundary, which would also have increased the number of residential units and provided considerable benefits to the scheme as a whole. The owners of this property were, in principle, prepared to sell but no site investigation had been undertaken.

The Council's development brief specified that there was a need for low to medium cost housing within this inner city area and that proposals should provide traditional housing with private gardens and car parking of two spaces per dwelling. Unnecessary through routes should be avoided, whilst taking advantage of the riverside location.

A number of developers had looked at this site, both before and after the issue of the development brief. Market research indicated a high demand for rented accommodation but an insufficient demand for owner-occupation. An approach was made to the City Council in 1998 to seek their support for an application for 'gap funding' from the English Partnerships Investment Fund. The intending developer was a locally based company, which at that time was developing a nearby site with new homes for rent. The company had a considerable waiting list for rental properties and wished to carry out a similar rental scheme on this site, however, the anticipated cost of remediation and the site owner's price expectations meant that the development would not be viable without public sector funding.

The Council's response was that it wished to 'encourage owner-occupation in this area' and it was not prepared to support this proposal as there was 'an over supply of rented accommodation in the Charlestown area in both the private and public rented sectors'. This was despite the policy statement in the brief that the Council will continue to encourage the provision of affordable housing, in accordance with PPG3 - *'Affordable housing includes housing for rent, shared ownership, or low cost sale.... The need for affordable housing in Salford reflects the increasing levels of house prices and rents in recent years, the increasing level of owner occupation and the large number of people on the Council's accommodation list.'*

Due to the high cost of remediating this site, it would only have been possible to undertake a residential development with financial assistance from English Partnerships. In order to obtain funding, it would be necessary to obtain the support of the Council. As this had been refused, the proposed developer abandoned the scheme. The site owner needed to maximise the proceeds obtained from selling the site, in order to repay bank borrowings and a relocation loan from the local authority. The price initially offered by the intending developer was £300,000, or more than £175,000 per hectare (£70,000 per acre). This offer reflected the generally run-down local environment and the industrial nature of the site, but was made before the full extent of the contamination became known.

At least two other house builders subsequently considered developing the site with housing for sale, or with a 'mixed tenure' scheme but also concluded that, without grant assistance, it would remain financially unviable to develop. Taking account of the rather more serious nature of the contamination and the Council's redevelopment policy for the area, the site owner was unable to obtain an adequate offer for the site and the company went into receivership.

Comment

The first intrusive investigation of this site was clearly not sufficient to fully explore the likelihood of contamination being present. It was, however, constrained by the presence of existing buildings and carried out without the benefit of an historical desk study. Both of these points were recognised by the investigator who recommended a detailed desk study and, after demolition, further sampling and testing in order to establish in detail the pattern of contamination across the site.

KEY POINTS

- There is a need for local authorities to consider very carefully the possibility that land allocated for housing development in local plans or UDP's may not be developable for such purposes without significant inputs of public sector funding - which may not be available.

- Site owners may appear to seek unrealistically high prices for 'previously used' land but, in practice, they may be caught in a situation where 'high values', ascribed to properties whilst they were in full economic use, and used to underpin the company's balance sheet, may not be achievable once the previous use ceases.

- Physical constraints on site investigations will often exist and, in many cases, it may not be possible for these to be resolved until such time as the existing buildings have been demolished. If the intending developer is to undertake the further investigations it may be necessary to enter into an option agreement, or a conditional contract with provision for the purchase price to be renegotiated in the light of results obtained from those investigations.

DETR Industry Profiles: Chemical works: rubber processing works; Textile works and dye works

---

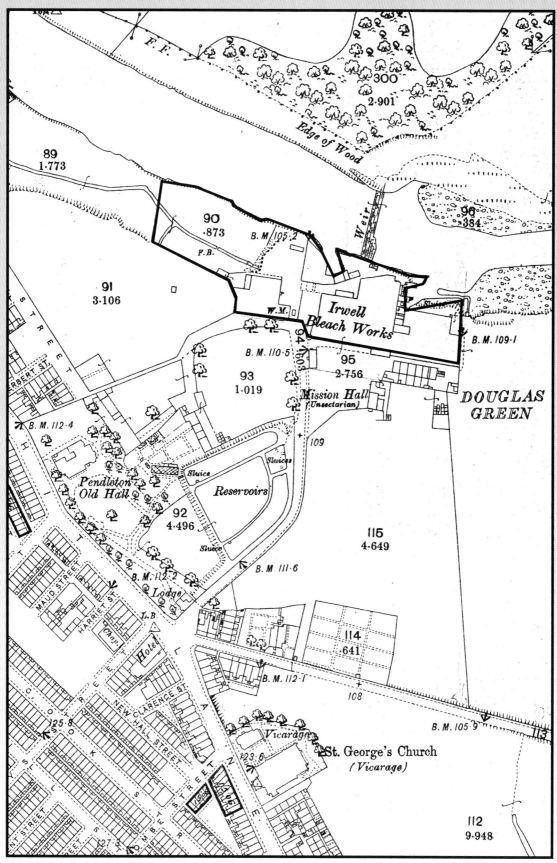

Figure 5.1 Irwell Bleach Works, Salford, in 1893, showing the weir adjacent to the site and what appears to be a small dock below the weir

6. *Dye works, chemical works, railway, cattle pens, coal merchants, electric lightbulb manufacture, oil depot, scrap yard*

- ON-SITE SORTING, MIXING AND RE-DISTRIBUTION OF MATERIAL
- HOUSING WITH PRIVATE GARDENS, MANAGED HOUSING, NON-RESIDENTIAL DEVELOPMENT AND LEISURE OPEN SPACE

Location:	Bede Island North, Leicester
Size of site:	11 hectares
Contaminants:	heavy metals, hydrocarbons, PCBs, methane
Potential receptors:	building workers, occupiers, surface and ground waters

This was a mixed use development, part of which included housing for Leicester Housing Association. The site is approximately one kilometre south-west of Leicester City Centre. The River Soar forms the western site boundary and the Grand Union Canal the eastern boundary. The site is relatively flat and is bordered to the west by industrial units and housing. It had been occupied by a number of different industrial activities - see Table 6.1 and the map extract from 1912, Figure 6.1.

Bede Island North was identified by Leicester City Challenge as a priority area for urban regeneration, comprising six development zones - retail, private residential, housing association, science park and public park. The site investigation and remediation of the entire site was undertaken as part of the City Challenge project and was gap funded by English Partnerships. Nicholls Colton and Partners undertook a preliminary site investigation at the site between March 1993 and January 1995. A total of 177 exploratory holes were excavated during this time.

The preferred developers chosen for the Bede Island North development by Leicester City Challenge were William Davis Ltd and Wilson Bowden Properties Ltd. In February 1995 ACER Consultants Ltd. (now part of Hyder Plc) was instructed to undertake an interim appraisal of contamination issues.

Table 6.1 Former site uses

Site Activity	Major Potential Associated Contaminants
Dye works. Established on site between 1886 and 1904. Dyers and finishers, specialising in hose and half hose, socks, wool(cotton) and cashmere fabric. Ceased operations between 1925 and 1936.	Metal and organic chemical based compounds. Organic chemicals derived from coal tar; e.g. aniline and anthracene.
Redline Motor Spirit Co.Ltd (The) Oil Merchants. Ceased operations between 1941 and 1957.	Petroleum based hydrocarbons Diesel fuel oil Mineral oil
London and North Eastern Railway (L&NER) Yard. Goods shed, Engine Shed. Maintenance and decommissioning work. Established between 1886 and 1904. Ceased operations at the site between 1957 and 1963	Mineral oils Asbestos De-greasing compounds Diesel fuels
Brico Commercial Chemical Company Limited. Established at the site between 1938 and 1941. Ceased operations at the site between 1957 and 1963.	Nature of activity presently unknown Bleach probably used
Electric Light Works. Manufacture of light bulbs, strip lights and or fittings. Established on site between 1886 and 1904	Metals, including mercury Glass waste
Coal Merchants	Coal
Scrap Metal Processing 1950's to present day	Metals Mineral oils Petrol Hydrocarbons and Diesel fuel Radioactive materials PCB's
Cattle pens Established on site between 1886 and 1904	Biological hazards

ACER recommended a further site investigation. This was carried out between May and June 1995, consisting of a further 35 boreholes, 21 trial pits and 8 probe holes with associated chemical and engineering testing, gas monitoring, water sampling and interpretation. On an average basis, the combined site investigations equated to a 26m x 26m grid over the whole site. This complied with guidance in British Standards Institution DD 175 and Contaminated Land Research Report CLR4.

Borehole records reveal that there is typically 4 metres of fill material overlying alluvial clay deposits. The alluvial clay deposits rest upon a layer of sand and gravel 0.5 metres to 4m thick (av.1metre) overlying Mercia Mudstone bedrock.

Groundwater measurements suggested the presence of two ground water regimes beneath the site, namely;

- discontinuous perched water in the fill

- a confined aquifer within the sand and gravel, which was in hydraulic continuity with the river and/or the canal

The degree of soil contamination was assessed with reference to ICRCL Guidance Note 59/83. The gas monitoring results were interpreted in accordance with the guidance given in Waste Management Paper No 27, 1991. This document gives a trigger value of 1% by volume for methane and 1.5% by volume for carbon dioxide in buildings.

The soil chemical test data revealed that the contamination threshold triggers were exceeded by the contaminants in Table 6.2.

Table 6.2 Contaminants identified on site

Contaminant	Number of Samples	Number of samples exceeding threshold concentration	Number of samples exceeding trigger concentration
Arsenic	288	25	
Cadmium	288	40	
Lead	288	13 (Open Space)	40 (houses)
Mercury	288	23 (gardens)	
Soluble Boron	288		173 (plants)
Copper + Nickel + Zinc	288	48	
Cyclohexane Extractable Matter	108	18	
Toluene Extractable Matter	108	1	
Total Phenols	289	17 (all uses)	
Polycyclic Aromatic Hydrocarbons	291		47 (domestic gardens)
Mineral Oils	58	58	6
Volatile Organic Compounds	5	1	
Semi Volatile Organic Compounds	8	8	0
Polychlorinated Biphenyls	279		26

Water samples taken from the upper (perched water) and the lower (groundwater) standpipes in 10 boreholes distributed across the site identified no particular trends other than that mineral oil contamination was evident across the whole site. Methane was recorded in concentrations above the 1% by volume trigger level at various times in 13 of 88 standpipes monitored, with three monitoring points exhibiting a trend greater than 10% by volume. The carbon dioxide levels beneath most of the site exceeded 1.5% by volume. Beneath significant areas of the site, carbon dioxide levels were recorded at and above 5% by volume. Both of these gases were considered to be of 'natural' origin rather than from the decomposition of buried putrescible waste.

Due to the time scale of the site reclamation programme, and the nature and volumes of contaminated material, a civil engineering solution was deemed to be the most appropriate. For reclamation purposes the site was divided into four principal areas. The planned end use of Area 1 was housing units with individual gardens, Area 2 comprised parkland and landscaped areas, Area 3 includes a science park, retail outlets and student accommodation, and Area 4 is the existing Great Central Way. The sensitivity of Area 1 was considered *high* whilst that of the remaining areas was considered to be *intermediate* to *low*.

Two separate reclamation standards were developed, with a standard for Area 1 and a standard for Areas 2 and 3. No reclamation works were proposed in Area 4.

The proposed reclamation scheme aimed to minimise off-site disposal by sorting, mixing and redistributing about the upper 1m to 2m of fill by inversion and/or translation. Inversion means bringing deeper, less contaminated, material to the surface and translation is the moving and re-use of material about the site taking into account relative sensitivities. Only material that exceeded trigger levels for the most sensitive end uses - i.e. housing - was removed from site. It was estimated that some 37,000 tonnes of contaminated material and an additional 13,500 tonnes of uncontaminated material would need to be removed from site.

In the housing area all material was excavated to a depth of 1.7m below final topsoil level and screened to assess its suitability for re-use elsewhere on the development. A capillary breaklayer consisting of 0.2m of crushed concrete was placed across this area. The site was then back filled with inert topsoil following construction of building foundations. Due to the fact that all contaminants would be removed from the residential area it was envisaged that there would be no special requirements in terms of service trenches etc.

All work undertaken was in accordance with health and safety legislation, measures included decontamination units provided for workers on site. A resident engineer supervised the works. Samples taken from Area 1 were analysed in order to determine their contamination status and suitability to be re-used elsewhere on the site. All works, including the movement of material, were fully documented.

The development for Leicester Housing Association consists of 73 terraced units. Sixty-two of the properties were for rent and 11 were for shared ownership. William Davis Ltd built the homes on behalf of the housing association.

The main issue in design terms related to the levels of methane and carbon dioxide. Leicester City Council required suitable venting measures to be incorporated into the design for each unit and required an alarm system to be fitted.

The agreed solution was to use a series of gas membranes incorporated into a reinforced raft membrane. At the base of the foundation a Geofin dispersal layer was attached to a Geofin gas vent box. The raft was then encapsulated with a Geoflex Geofoil gas membrane effectively creating two layers of membrane. The design incorporated an alarm system that comprised two sensors in each unit (one under the stairs and one on the first floor).

The alarm system is monitored 24 hours a day at Leicester Housing Association headquarters. If the gas reaches excessive levels the alarm sounds and a response team goes to the development. Such a system can be difficult to maintain and there have been instances where the alarms have been activated by such things as chip pan fires. No time limit was set by the local authority as to when the use of the alarm system could be discontinued. Therefore this will be a continued cost and maintenance for the housing association, which could continue far into the future.

Comment

Despite removal of contaminated material from the residential area, problems of continued gassing still remained. The venting measures installed beneath the homes in most developments of this sort may have been adequate without the alarm system. It may therefore have been over cautious of the local authority to require the additional precaution of a 24 hour alarm system which needs continued maintenance and in many cases may preclude the development of such homes for private sale. There is also the need to agree a post development period for the continued monitoring of gas flows.

KEY POINTS

*   In a mixed used scheme there is the potential to re-use material on another part of the site that would be unsuitable for residential use.

*   In the case of a gassing site it is important to identify the cost implications for different solutions and possible maintenance implications.

*   Identify the requirement of the local authority and any conditions for the continued monitoring of gassing levels.

*   The requirement for a site wide alarm system may preclude the development of homes for private sale.

DETR Industry Profiles: Chemical works: fine chemicals manufacturing works: inorganic chemicals manufacturing works; Engineering works: electrical and electronic equipment manufacturing works; Waste recycling, treatment and disposal sites: metal recycling sites; Railway land.

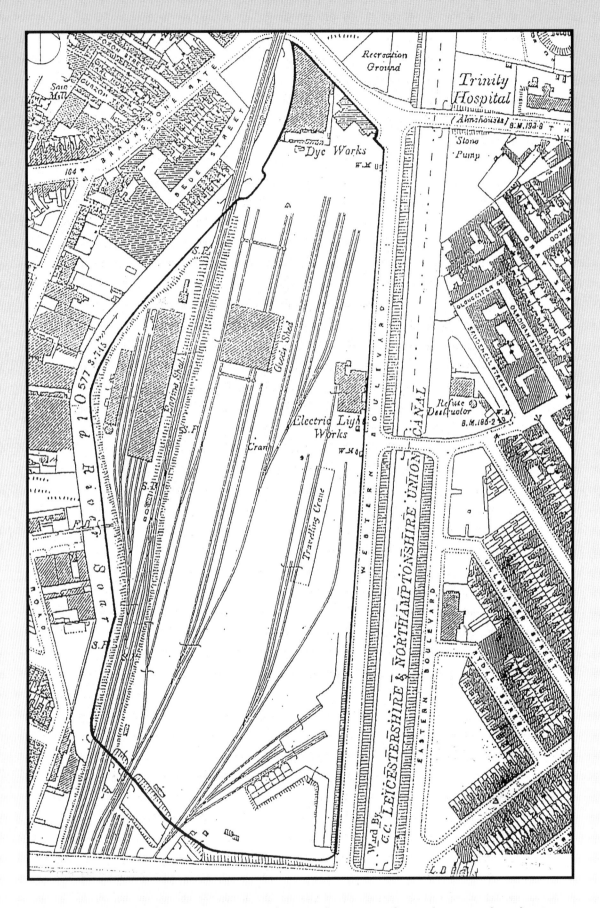

Figure 6.1 *Bede Island, Leicester, in 1912, showing the variety of uses that existed on the site*

7. Iron works, lime kiln dock, timber yard, town gas works

- PARTIAL REMOVAL, ON-SITE CONTAINMENT AND CAPPING
- LUXURY APARTMENTS, PLUS COMMERCIAL USE

Location:	'Western Wharf' - Graham's Yard, Brandon's Shed and Brandon's Yard, Anchor Road, Bristol
Size of site:	1.09 hectares
Contaminants:	heavy metals, sulphates, ammoniacal nitrogen
Potential receptors:	building workers, surface water

This case study development site forms part of the Canon's Marsh in the Harbourside regeneration area, the major portion of which is the former gasworks, situated in close proximity to the city centre. After gas production on the site ceased, part of the land was used for gas storage until it was decommissioned in 1998 but a large part had lain derelict for many years.

The Western Wharf site is to be developed by Beaufort Western Ltd., who intend to carry out a mixed use development, comprising residential apartments and leisure use. Part of the site is already owned by the developer, and any reclamation will be its responsibility, but the eastern part of the site - Brandon's Yard - is owned by BGPlc (British Gas), which will be responsible for remediation works in this area. Figure 7.1 is a context plan and elevation drawing, showing massing to the Floating Harbour. The site is bounded on the north by Anchor Road and on the south by Bristol's historic Floating Harbour.

A desk study revealed that, in 1884, the western part of the site - Graham's Yard and Brandon's Shed - was occupied by a foundry (New Quay Iron Works) which included a dock (Lime Kiln Dock), later a dry dock. Brandon's Yard formed part of a large town gas works and includes two listed buildings, together with the base of a former gasholder.

By 1930 the Lime Kiln Dock had been filled in and the ironworks had been removed. The western part of the site was in use as a timber yard, this use continued until 1999.

In January 1999, archaeologists from Bristol City Museum examined the site, opening it up with large trenches, in both the former dry dock area and through the concrete slab in the eastern part of the site. This examination confirmed the presence of made ground. "In common with many other areas of low lying ground in Bristol, throughout the development of the city, ground levels would have been raised by general infilling of material, which would have included ash and clinker, building rubble and the like."

(Hyder, 1999). Ash and clinker are potential sources of elevated heavy metal concentrations. Heavy metals and other trace elements are naturally present in coal, (and other raw materials used in association with coal burning), and become concentrated in the ash and clinker residues.

The made ground discovered by the archaeologists comprised a dark brown clayey-sandy soil matrix with ash, brick and slate fragments, consistent with the type of fill material found in other parts of the city. There was some evidence of hydrocarbon contamination in the eastern part of the site, evidenced by excavation odours which dispersed after a day or two. The presence of hydrocarbon contamination was confirmed by the later site investigation.

The natural geology of the site, below the fill material, is Estuarine Alluvium (from the Pleistocene era), overlying Quartzitic Sandstone. The solid geology beneath the site is classified as a non-aquifer by the British Geological Survey, nevertheless, one licensed abstraction is situated 270 metres from the site.

The harbour wall of the Floating Harbour forms the southern boundary of the development site. The Floating Harbour is a 'man-made' non-tidal body of water, formed in the late 19th Century by impounding the River Avon, the main flow of which was diverted to bypass the dock along the New Cut.

The environmental consultants' report confirmed that no contaminative activities remained on site and a site investigation was undertaken to determine the extent of any soil and groundwater contamination. Leachate testing was also undertaken. This is an important part of the site investigation process but is often overlooked.

Elevated concentrations of arsenic, copper, lead, nickel and zinc were found in soil samples in the western part of the site. A possible source of arsenic and copper contamination could have been copper-chromium-arsenic wood preservatives (see Syms, 1999, p40) but, as elevated concentrations of chromium were not present, this was considered to be unlikely. The most probable source of the metal contaminants was therefore considered to be the foundry and ship building/repairing operations which preceded the timber yard use.

Elevated concentrations of sulphate, principally to the east of the former dock, were attributed to general building rubble in the made ground. Cadmium and lead were found in the perched water in the infilled dock and were assumed to have either leached from the fill materials, or to have come from highway runoff.

Ammoniacal nitrogen was recorded in four locations in the western part of the site and was attributed to contaminants having migrated from the adjoining gasworks site. The eastern part of the site, which formed part of the old gasworks, is understood to be the most contaminated part of the BG Plc land.

A development brief was prepared by Bristol City Council Planning Department for the regeneration of Bristol Harbourside and the 'Implementation Phase' was approved by the Planning, Transport and Development Committee of the City Council, in July 1998. The Harbourside covers 27 hectares of former dock and industrial land, of which this site forms part.

Commercial and industrial use of the Floating Harbour had declined over many years, with resulting dereliction of the adjoining land and buildings, although there had been an increase in leisure activities. Development of the Lloyds Bank (now Lloyds TSB) headquarters building in 1989 was seen as a catalyst for the regeneration of the area and prompted a review of planning policy.

The Council's objectives are "to achieve regeneration of the area with development designed for a diverse and balanced range of uses which will ensure a level of vitality and activity appropriate to this prestigious city centre site" (Bristol City Council, 1998). These objectives were to be met inter alia by securing major cultural and leisure facilities, including further development of the principal leisure functions of the waterfront and by providing new opportunities for housing. Thus the proposed mixed residential and leisure uses proposed for the site are in accordance with the policies outlined in the development brief.

Planning permission has been granted for remediation of the entire gasworks site but, at the time the case study research was undertaken, planning permission had been refused for the mixed use redevelopment of the main gasworks site.

The City Council has resolved to grant planning permission for the Western Wharf development, subject to the developer entering into an agreement under section 106 of the Town & Country Planning Act 1990 but a small part of the gasworks site, Brandons Yard, forms part of the Beaufort development site. This land cannot be redeveloped until it has been remediated as part of the comprehensive programme of work for the gasworks site, notwithstanding the fact that it is physically separated from the main site by Gas Ferry Lane (see Figure 7.1).

Bristol City Council's Planning Department wished to see the leisure and residential developments dealt with as a single application, so as to avoid 'cherry picking' of the site, leaving listed buildings in a state of disrepair. The joint view of the Planning and Environmental Health Departments is that the whole of the gasworks site should be remediated under a single contract, so as to avoid cross contamination, migration and air-borne contaminant transmission, which might arise if the site is remediated on a piecemeal basis. Whichever view is correct, and the truth is likely to be a mix of both, commencement of the leisure element of the Western Wharf redevelopment has been delayed.

The proposal now agreed involves the phased remediation and redevelopment of the site, which would allow the residential development to be undertaken on the western half of the site, with the leisure development, including restoration of the listed buildings, on the Brandon's Yard area to be postponed until such time as the whole of the gasworks site has been remediated.

The remediation methodology proposed for the western part of the site involves reducing the site level by 1.5 metres, through the removal of contaminated soil and its disposal to landfill, down to the level of the highest part of the Lime Kiln Dock walls. The dock walls would be exposed and the dock area itself landscaped as a central feature to the residential development. This would also provide a vista through the site, from Anchor Road, to the ss Great Britain and the associated visitor centre on the opposite side of the Floating Harbour.

Contaminated spoil from the residential site would be moved within the development area and deposited in the base of the former gasholder in the Brandon's Yard part of the site. Approximately 3,000 cubic metres of contaminated material will need to be moved and it is estimated that the gasholder base has capacity for around 8,000 cubic metres.

Reducing the level of the residential development site will enable basement car parking to be provided under the two apartment buildings. The ground floors of the new apartments will thus be approximately 1.5 metres above the existing ground level.

As this report went to press a draft Sec. 106 Agreement had been issued. This is far more complex than expected because the Council takes the view that it cannot covenant in the Agreement with itself. Therefore Beaufort has to take on primary liability for complex leisure and infrastructure payments, even though it will receive an indemnity from the Council in the separate land agreement. Progress on the adjoining main Canon's Marsh site has slowed down somewhat. Following the refusal of a Planning Application by Crest, the Council has admitted that a fresh approach is required, but the process of granting Crest an extension of its contract was delayed by an application for Judicial Review, issued by a resident of Bristol. Also, an alternative scheme has been submitted for planning permission even though the developer concerned has no interest in the land.

Comment

This case study illustrates problems that can be encountered when sites are in several ownerships and where a number of different developers are involved. A 'stale mate' situation can soon evolve. Although the site could, in practice, be remediated and redeveloped in parts the Council has prevented this. In the late 1990's the site might, but for the City Council's opposition, have been included in the area controlled by the Bristol Development Corporation. English

Partnerships have provided gap funding for infrastructure which will be recovered as the development proceeds.

This is a unique waterside city centre development area, offering a redevelopment opportunity not seen in Bristol since the post-war era. Arguably, the urban planners' scope was severely restricted by the construction of the new Lloyds Bank headquarters on the most prominent part of the area, with its frontage dominating the prime waterside location and the back of its building facing the, as yet, undeveloped Canons Marsh area which is in close proximity to Bristol's historic cathedral.

The significant delays in bringing this area forward for redevelopment - which have affected development of the Western Wharf site, are attributable to:-

- *the time taken for the major landowners to come to agreement;*

- *strong local feeling about how the site should be developed which was not taken into account in the planning process and which resulted in the emergence of an alternative scheme;*

- *the planning process;*

- *environmental/contamination issues.*

KEY POINTS

- Explore the possibility of government funding to 'kick-start' such sites.

- Look at the possibility of using or threatening CPO powers to assemble complex sites such as this.

- Take full account of local views in a consultative process prior to a planning application and ensure a good pathway of communication between all interested parties.

- Do not underestimate the costs of delays caused by planning problems, which may involve protracted negotiations.

- Keep in mind that, while such problems are resolved, contamination may worsen, particularly if it is of migratory nature.

- Costs will, almost inevitably, increase and liabilities may change in response to new legislation.

DETR Industry Profiles: Gas works, coke works and other coal carbonisation plants; Metal manufacturing, refining and finishing works: iron and steelworks; Timber treatment works.

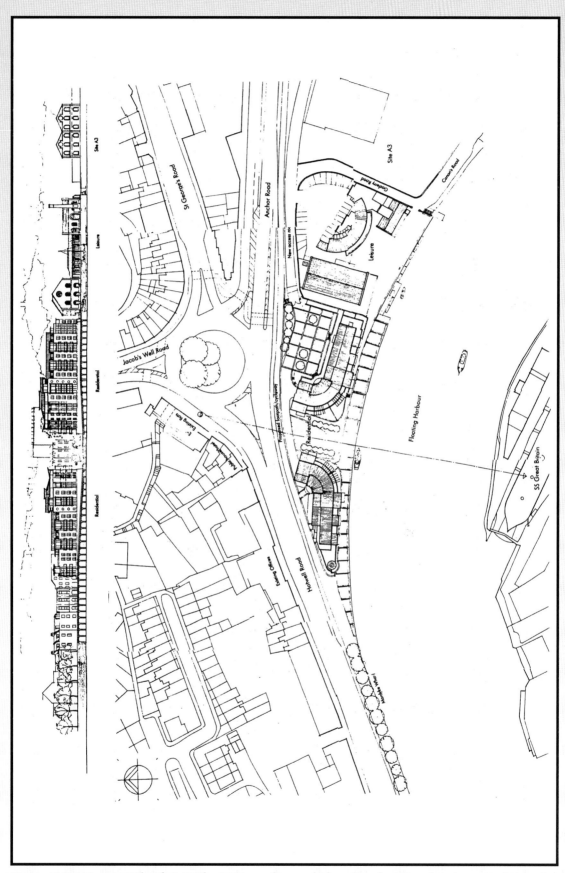

Figure 7.1 Western Wharf, Bristol - Context plan and elevation drawing showing massing to the Floating Harbour

1

1   Contaminated fill material and poor access
    at Salford

2   New homes for rent, showing gas venting
    stacks and cowls, Bede Island, Leicester

3   Children's play area, Bede Island, Leicester

2

3

4

5

6

7

4   Former lime kiln, timber yard and gas
    works, Floating Harbour, Bristol

5   Gasferry Lane, dividing Western Wharf
    from the main gas works site

6   New houses under construction, former
    petrol station and garage, Fairford,
    Gloucestershire

7   New 'cottage style' house, Fairford,
    Gloucestershire

8

9

10

8   Fixing cut-off wall to prevent
     recontamination, Faiford
9   Housing association development, former
     gas works rail yard, Beckton, East London
10   Housing association development, former
     gas works rail yard, Beckton, East London

11

12

13

14

11   New homes under construction, showing
     installation of geotextile membrane,
     Beckton, East London
12   Show home and sales office, Beckton,
     East London
13   New flats, Northwich, Cheshire
14   New homes for sale, Northwich, Cheshire

8. Landfill

- SORTING, MIXING AND RE-DISTRIBUTION OF MATERIAL, GAS PROTECTION MEASURES
- HOUSING ASSOCIATION, RENTED AND FOR SALE, CHILDREN'S HOME

Location:	**Bismarck Street, York**
Size of site:	**0.514 hectares**
Contaminants:	**methane, heavy metals**
Potential receptors:	**occupiers and building structures**

This development is located in a low-lying area of York close to the River Ouse. The site had been licensed to accept construction waste during the period 1980 to 1988 and had been filled to a depth of approximately 4 metres. Historical records also show that approximately 110 metres from the Northeast boundary of Bismarck Street there had been an unlicensed tip that had been filled during the period 1932-1948.

After the development site ceased to be used as a tip it was grassed over and used as public open space. The site was owned by City of York Council, which was keen to see it redeveloped for housing. The City Council was aware of the past use of the site and was concerned about the possible presence of methane, although it considered the site to be low risk due to the fact that it had only been licensed to accept construction waste.

The development was undertaken for the Joseph Rowntree Housing Trust (JRHT) by Denne Construction Ltd and consisted of 11 houses, 8 flats and a children's home. Six of the homes were for shared ownership sale and the rest were rented housing to be occupied by local authority nominees.

In December 1997 JRHT and the City of York commissioned a site investigation by Norwest Holst. This initially consisted of 4 boreholes (3 shallow and 1 deep) and 8 trial pits. The investigation revealed that the made ground consisted of clay, gravel, stone, brick rubble and ash. Occasional pockets of organic alluvium were found in borehole 2 (see site plan, Figure 8.1) but otherwise no significant deposits of organic matter were found. Natural ground, consisting of layers of clay, sand and gravel, was found below the fill. No organic matter was found in the natural ground.

Planning permission for residential development was granted in March 1998 subject to a condition stipulating that "development shall not commence until a site investigation and assessment of possible gas emission within the site has been carried out" and "any proposed remedial measures to prevent any gas causing a hazard either during the course of development or during subsequent use of the site, has been submitted and approved in writing by the Assistant Director (Planning and Environment)".

As part of the investigation, gas monitoring was undertaken. At first, concentrations of methane were below threshold levels (1.0% by volume) but in May 1998, two of the boreholes showed elevated levels of methane of up to 70.4% by volume. Carbon dioxide readings were all below 1.5% by volume. Although the methane concentrations were high, flow rates were low at around 1.4 litres per hour. The overall volume of gas produced was small but, if confined, it could be potentially explosive.

The discovery of methane occurred just two weeks before JRHT was due to sign contracts for the site. Had the methane been discovered after this time then the cost of remedial measures would not have been reflected in the land price.

Development was delayed while further readings were taken. A further five boreholes were sunk and monitored by Norwest Holst. The highest readings (71.5% & 66.5% methane by volume) came from borehole 2 in July 1998 after a period of heavy rain increased the ground water level. High readings (18.2%) were also recorded in borehole A, the deep borehole in close proximity to borehole 2. The other shallow boreholes showed much reduced levels of methane.

Waste Management Paper No 27 (1991) recommends that dwelling houses should not be built where methane and carbon dioxide levels exceed 1% and 1.5% by volume respectively. This could have led to the possibility that the Council might not allow the development to go ahead. The Council was very keen to see the development go ahead and agreed to joint fund further site investigations. A specialist team from Stanger Science and Environment was appointed to advise on possible reclamation schemes.

The consultants believed that the gas was probably migrating from off-site and had been confined at depth until the natural clay seal had been punctured by boreholes 2 and A. Clay was not so prevalent to the south of the site allowing methane to rise to the surface and dissipate naturally. Further flow readings were taken which revealed that after initial high readings from boreholes 2 and A the flow rate dramatically reduced.

Stangers looked at three possible remedial measures that could allow the development to proceed. The City of York had originally wished JRHT to install an automated alarm system to all the properties. This was not the preferred option of either JRHT or the consultants, as these systems require continued maintenance and in cannot be guaranteed that the work will be done in the future. In particular, they are not suitable where houses are to be sold. Possible alternative remedial schemes were:

• Interception Trench - with a need to be monitored for 1 year - effectiveness not guaranteed - not considered to be viable.

- Passive (natural) Venting System - these tend to be used where lower levels of methane present - but could be suitable.

- Mechanical (Active) Venting System - safest - not subject to vagaries of weather - costly to install and potential maintenance problems.

The finished development used a passive gas ventilation system comprising a granular blanket with periscope vents around the perimeter of the dwellings. This was upgraded to provide a continuous void under the building footprint by use of a Geofin GDS 40 geocomposite under the raft slab (See Figure 8.2). The geocomposite allows the methane to ventilate into the atmosphere through a system of perimeter gas collection pipes to vertical stack risers positioned around the building perimeter. The vented voids of the raft foundations are connected to external air by periscope vents passing through the edge beams of the raft. A gas proof membrane was provided above the raft protected by an overlying screed.

Other concerns of the City Council related to the ability of the wind to move the methane under certain weather conditions - low or nil wind. This was resolved by placing aspiromatic cowls on top of the venting system.

By reference to ICRCL threshold level for domestic gardens and allotments the site had slightly elevated levels of arsenic towards the northern boundary of the site. This contamination was not considered to be a serious problem and was resolved during development as the site level had to be raised by 1.5 metres to deal with flood conditions. The contaminated material was mixed with clean material and spread across the site, thereby diluting the contamination below ICRCL threshold level.

Following a delay of six months the development contractor started on site in January 1999. The additional remediation increased the total costs by £90,000, effectively reducing the land value to nil. The remediation work was supervised by the environmental consultant and inspected by JRHT's contract administrator and the Trust's 'in-house' Clerk of Works, as well as by the insurer's inspector and the local authority's building control officer.

Construction phase monitoring and post-construction monitoring have shown methane readings to be extremely low. These readings have been taken every two weeks for a period of four months, with a minimum monitoring period of 12 months.

The homes are insured by Zurich and, for the properties that are being sold, a copy of the consultants report has been forwarded to the purchaser's solicitor. Collateral warranties (to be provided by the consultants) were investigated by JRHT but were deemed to be too expensive. The development was completed in February 2000 and the homes were occupied by May of the same year.

Comment

This development had similar problems to that described in Chapter 6 although much higher concentrations of methane were recorded. The solution used in this development did not use an alarm system, although on-going monitoring is still a maintenance issue.

The high levels of methane were only discovered after an extended period of monitoring. Had it been discovered after signing a contract of intent JRHT could have been liable for the entire cost of remedial measures. It should therefore be recommended that clauses are included in any land transaction to take account of this. Soil mixing and effective dilution of the elevated arsenic levels provided an alternative cost effective method to excavation and removal.

KEY POINTS

- Whilst it is not always possible, it is preferable to monitor a potentially gassing site over a period of time and weather conditions.

- Examine contracts of intent and build clauses into contract where contamination might be an issue.

- Identify different solutions of dealing with methane and continued maintenance of such systems.

- Require time limits to be set by regulators in relation to any post-development monitoring.

> *DETR Industry Profiles: Waste recycling, treatment and disposal sites: landfills and other waste treatment or waste disposal sites.*

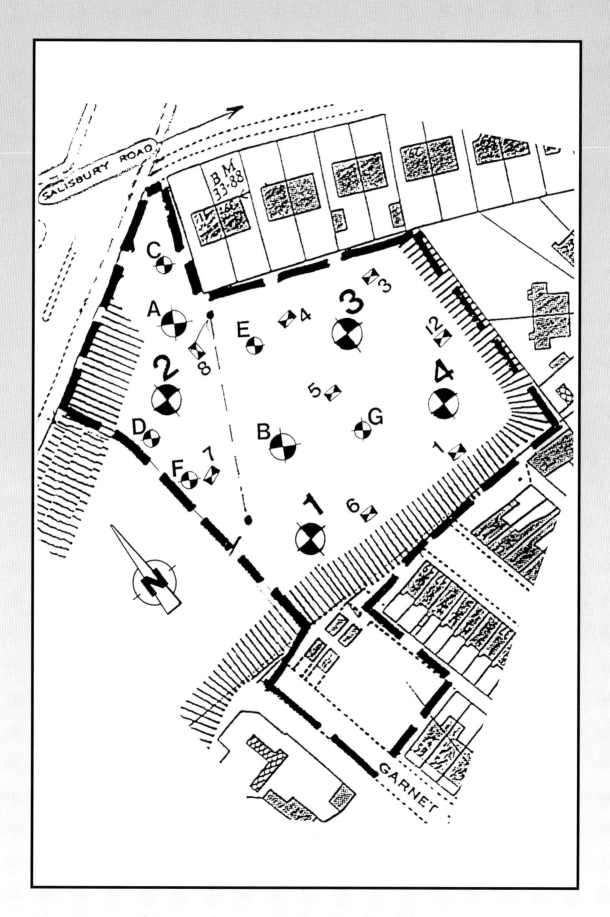

Figure 8.1 Bismarck Street, York, approximate locations of boreholes

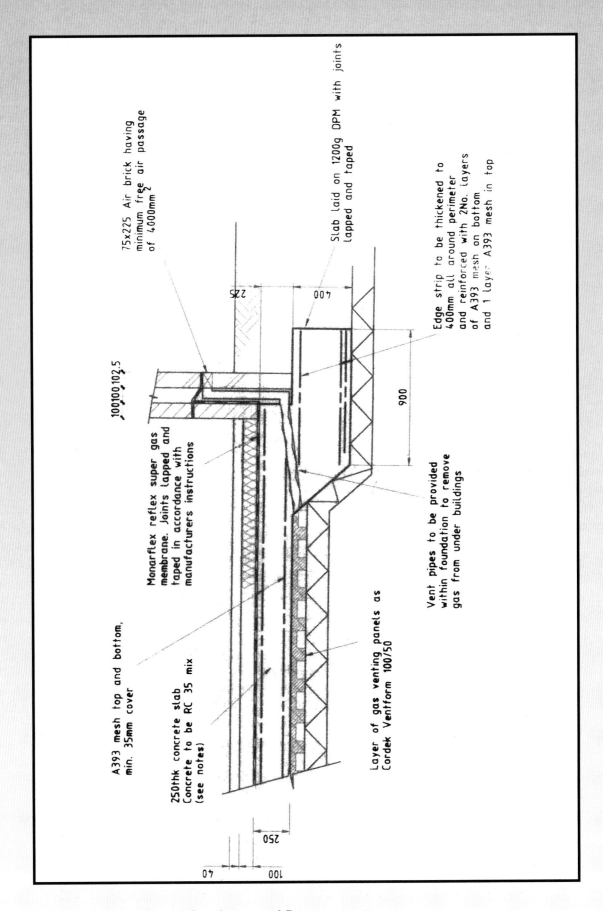

Figure 8.2 Section through foundations and floor construction

9. *Petrol filling station and motor vehicle workshops*

- BIO-REMEDIATION AND PART OFF-SITE DISPOSAL.
- DETACHED EXECUTIVE.

Location:	**'Milton Reach', former Busby's Garage and petrol filling station, Fairford, Gloucestershire**
Size of site:	**0.25 hectares**
Contaminants:	**hydrocarbons, heavy metals**
Potential receptors:	**ground and surface waters, occupiers, building workers**

A redevelopment by Beaufort Western Ltd., in a sensitive ground and surface water environment located in a Cotswold village. The development comprises six 'cottage' homes, built in Cotswold style to blend with the surrounding area. Construction was nearing completion at the time of the case studies research.

Prior to redevelopment the site was a petrol filling station and motor vehicle workshop, including a dwellinghouse occupied by the garage owner. The developer identified the potential of the site for residential development and undertook a formal demand study. The land was purchased from the garage owner but the developer was unable to agree terms for the dwellinghouse, which was excluded from the transaction.

Located close to the centre of the village, with a frontage to Milton Street, the eastern boundary of the site is formed by the River Coln, which is categorised chemically as River Quality A by the Environment Agency - i.e. good water quality. The Environment Agency stipulated that a four metre wide access strip should be reserved along the river bank to allow for maintenance.

The planning authority would have been prepared to consider other uses for the site although, due to land values in the area, housing was considered inevitable. The site was not zoned or identified for any particular use in the local plan, as the Council, in drawing up the plan, had assumed that the garage use would continue.

The average river level is approximately one metre below the original site level of 85 metres AOD and there is a rapid flow southwards. The site is level and "may be subject to flooding with an estimated 100 year return period flood of 1 to 2 m. depth." (Komex Clarke Bond, 1997).

A desk study disclosed that, in 1886, much of Milton Street had been developed, with buildings on both sides of the road. Only the northern section of the site, i.e. that part nearest the road, had been developed and a gasworks was located approximately 150 metres south east of the site on the opposite (east) bank of the river.

The site had been further developed by 1903, with the construction of a smithy in the southern half. The smithy was still in existence in 1924 and by 1960 further development had taken place in the south east section of the site.

The British Geological Survey notes a landfill recorded as being within 60 metres to the west of the site. There are two surface water discharge consents, both relating to sewage effluent, within 1km of the site and three licensed groundwater abstractions points within 2km.

British Geological Survey map data show the site as being underlain by river terrace deposits, comprising mainly of gravels, with solid geology of the Middle Jurassic era, aged Great Oolite Series, outcroppings to the north of Fairford. These consist largely of Cornbrash, Forest marbles and great Oolite Limestone. (note: Cornbrash is a brown, fossiliferous non-oolitic, rubbly limestone with abundant shell debris and a marly matrix) Upper Jurassic Oxford Clay and Kellaway Beds outcrop to the south of Fairford.

The NRA (1992) classes the site as being on the boundary between a major aquifer and a non-aquifer. "A non-aquifer is a formation with negligible permeability that is regarded as containing insignificant quantities of groundwater. Major aquifers are highly permeable strata usually with a known or probable presence of significant fracturing. The gravel drift deposit covering the underlying strata would form a permeable boundary, thus enabling water to easily recharge the aquifers below." (Komex Clarke Bond, 1997).

This site lies on the southern edge of an extensive and highly productive aquifer, the interbeded clays can also cause local perched water tables and springs. Taken together with the proximity of the River Coln, there is the potential for contaminative activities, leaks from underground storage tanks and the disposal of wastes to cause harm to the water environment. Table 9.1 sets out the potential for environmental hazards from past activities on this site.

The environmental consultants concluded from their 'desk study' that significant risk was posed by the presence of underground storage tanks (USTs) on the site, due to the high probability that one or more of the tanks, or associated fuel lines may have leaked into the surrounding soils. The hazards were identified as being potentially harmful to the flora and fauna of the river, water abstractors downstream of the site and the occupiers of adjacent buildings due to the build-up of vapours. Other hazards were identified, associated with the former vehicle workshop, the vehicle wash, the former smithy and the off-site landfill.

Table 9.1 Potential environmental hazards

Potential sources of contamination at the Fairford site included: fuelling areas, workshops, a smithy and vehicle washing areas. Off-site sources of contamination included the recorded nearby landfill. The contaminants potentially present are listed below:

Fuelling areas

- Petroleum spirit: alcohols, ethers, organo-lead compounds, benzene, branched olefins, long chain aliphatic compounds, napthalenes, polycyclic aromatic hydrocarbons (PAHs);
- Petrol additives such as tetramethyllead (TML), methyl tertiary butyl ether (MTBE) etc.; and,
- Diesel (derv or gas oil): additives.

Workshops

- Metals and metal compounds: copper, zinc, lead, chromium, vanadium;
- Waste oil: polycyclic aromatic hydrocarbons (PAHs), heavy metals;
- Anti-freeze e.g. ethylene glycol
- Brake fluids e.g. polymerised glycols and ethers
- Solvents (non-chlorinated) e.g. white spirit, methanol, xylene, glycols, esters, ketones;
- Solvents (chlorinated) e.g. dichloromethane, trichloroethylene, etc.;
- Paints containing lead, zinc, esters, isocyanates, ketones;
- Thinners: glycol ethers; and;
- Inorganic compounds: asbestos, sulphur, isocyanates, battery acids.

Smithy

- metals, including; arsenic, antimony, barium, cadmium, chromium, copper, lead, manganese, nickel, tin and zinc;
- non-metals, including cyanides, chlorides, fluorides, phosphorus, sulphide, sulphates;
- acids, for example hydrochloric, phosphoric, sulphuric;
- alkalis, such as degreasants, ammoniacal liquors; and,
- organic substances; including oils, cleaning and degreasing fluids;

Vehicle wash areas

Detergent constituents: linear alkyl sulphonates, sodium carbonate, sodium silicate, sodium hydroxide, ethylene diamine tetraacetic acid (EDTA), nitriloacetic acid (NTA).

Landfill

- Metals, including arsenic, cadmium, chromium and copper;
- Non-metals, including cyanides, chlorides and sulphides;
- Acids and alkalis, for example hydrochloric acid;
- Organic substances, including oils, tarry wastes and PCBs;
- Biodegradable matter, e.g. household waste; and,
- Asbestos.

Source: Komex Clarke Bond 1997

Heavy metal contamination and hydrocarbon contamination, associated with the former smithy and the workshop drainage interceptor, were also identified as constraints on redevelopment. The fill material in trenches for underground utility pipes had the potential to provide a pathway through which contaminants might migrate and the close proximity of the River Coln suggested that dissolved phase hydrocarbons may have entered the river system. The consultants recommended that a full intrusive investigation be undertaken, to assess the soil contamination and with the object of removing the USTs.

The first phase of the intrusive investigation was conducted in March 1998 and comprised five boreholes, three of which were completed as shallow groundwater monitoring wells. It was not possible to excavate trial pits as much of the site was still covered by buildings and hardstandings. A second phase investigation was therefore undertaken in January 1999 approximately three months prior to commencement of the remediation work, comprising 16 trial pits and two further groundwater monitoring wells. The locations of the trial pits and groundwater monitoring wells from both phases of the investigation are shown in Figure 9.1.

Soil samples from each borehole in the first phase investigation were characterised on site by testing for hydrocarbon vapours using a Photo Ionisation Detector calibrated to isobutylene (benzene response factor 1.0). "The method employed is highly subjective, but does provide semi quantitative information on the vertical and lateral distribution of hydrocarbons across the site. These results were used to select one to two soil samples from each soil boring to characterise the horizons containing the highest contaminant concentrations." (Komex Clarke Bond 1998). Water samples were taken from each of the monitoring wells.

The soil and water samples were tested in the laboratory for total petroleum hydrocarbons (TPH), benzene, toluene, ethylbenzene and xylenes (BTEX) and/or for heavy metals. The intrusive investigation enabled discrete areas of contamination, requiring remedial treatment, to be identified.

The remediation methods selected comprised partial removal of the heavy metal contamination for off-site disposal and bio-remediation of the hydrocarbon contaminated soil, in nine windrows, Figure 9.2. Churngold, the contractor that carried out the remediation, had worked for the developer on previous projects and was selected on the basis of a negotiated contract.

The consultant felt that bio-remediation was a far better solution for dealing with the hydrocarbon contamination than other alternatives. The reasons given for this were that it dealt with the contamination 'once and for all', it minimised the use of fossil fuels, the cost was less than the alternatives and was better for 'public relations' in this sensitive area. It was also possible to re-use material from the site, by crushing concrete, instead of importing clean fill, thereby reducing vehicle movements, onto and off the site.

Although the remediation method was considered to be more environmentally acceptable, it was not problem free. Planning permission was not required for the remediation itself but the design and implementation of the work had to be approved in writing by the planning authority. Following meetings with the environmental health officer at Cotswold District Council and with the Environment Agency, it was agreed that a Waste Management Licence was not required for the remediation. Also, as the process used only normal construction site machinery and as the treated volume of material would be less than 400 cubic metres, a Mobile Plant Licence was not required.

With the exception of arsenic the regulatory authorities agreed the heavy metal remediation guidelines recommended by the consultant. In the case of arsenic, the Environmental Health Officer advocated using ICRCL "domestic garden" guidelines rather than those for "open spaces". The consultant agreed with this change as, due to the contaminant distribution, there was only a small incremental cost for use of the stricter criterion.

The first stage of the remediation involved the removal of underground storage tanks, breaking up and crushing the extensive over site concrete, for re-use on the site. This was done using a mobile 'city crusher', on tracks, with a noise level of only 60dBA. Local residents were advised before work commenced, dust suppression was achieved by water spraying and this phase of the remediation was completed in three days. The contractor received no complaints.

The bio-remediation of approximately 300 m³ of hydrocarbon contaminated material was achieved in four weeks. This fairly short treatment period was due to the fact that much of the hydrocarbon content was light fraction oils, which volatised on being exposed to air, leaving only the heavier oils to be treated. Material in the windrows was turned over during the treatment period using a tractor/rotovator. Nutrients were added in proper proportions and moisture content was carefully controlled. The remediation works were supervised and validated by the environmental consultant.

It is important to note that the remediation was carried out on the basis of rendering the site suitable for its intended use of residential development and to protect the River Coln. The works were undertaken with the full co-operation and agreement of the Environment Agency, to best standards of current practice, and were supervised by an experienced environmental consultant who compiled a detailed validation report of the remediation work (Komex 1999). Whilst the site is generally fit for purpose, it does not mean that there is no trace of hydrocarbon or other compounds in soil or groundwater at the site. Rather, these have been reduced to concentrations which the Environment Agency agree are below those that are suitable for the end use. The planning officer felt that the regulatory process could have been improved through early liaison between the planners, environmental health and the Environment Agency.

One issue of considerable concern to the developer, the environmental consultant and remediation contractor was that part of the garage site had been retained by the vendor of the site, this comprised the house and former petrol sales office in the north east corner of the site. Petrol pumps and underground storage tanks had been located in this area, adjacent to the road, and paraffin tanks and pump were located to the rear of the house.

Preventing the migration of contamination from this retained area to the development site was an important issue and was achieved by the installation of a low permeability membrane around the retained site. After the remediation works had been completed, and whilst the housing was under construction, the former petrol station house and sales office were sold for use as a private residence and the underground storage tanks were removed.

Strong interest was shown in the development and there was no apparent 'sales resistance' attributable to the former use of the site. In the view of the selling agent, former petrol station and garage uses are readily understood by prospective purchasers and should not detract from the saleability of a development.

Comment

This study demonstrates the importance of keeping local residents informed of site works that may cause noise or other inconvenience.

The developer also needs to be aware of adjacent sources of contamination and take appropriate steps to ensure that the remediated site does not become recontaminated.

KEY POINTS
- Bio-remediation was the selected method of decontaminating the site, based on cost and environmental factors. It was also very effective in terms of timescale.

> *DETR Industry Profile: Road vehicle fuelling, service and repair: garages and filling stations*

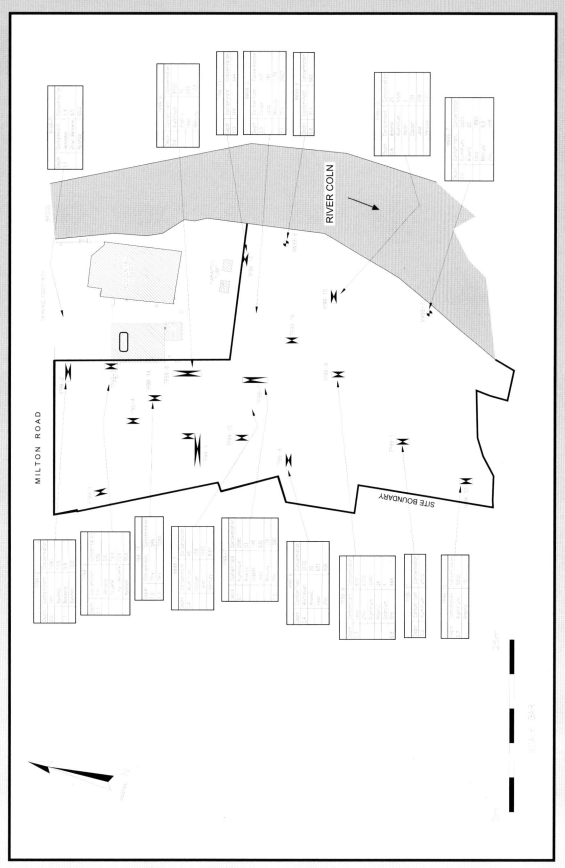

Figure 9.1 Site investigation, boreholes and trial pits, with contaminants located (all concentrations given in mg/kg)

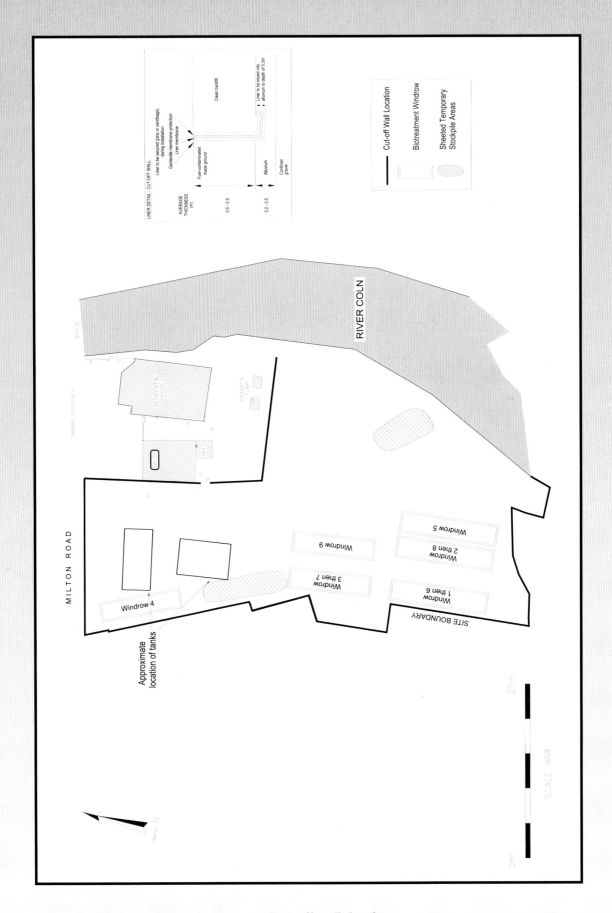

Figure 9.2 Bio-remediation windrows and cut-off wall details

10. *Rail yard forming part of a town gas works*

- COVER AND CONTAIN
- HOUSING ASSOCIATION RENTED AND PRIVATE FOR SALE, APARTMENTS AND HOUSES

Location:	**Winsor Park, Beckton, London E6**
Size of site:	**12 hectares**
Contaminants:	**gas works wastes**
Potential receptors:	**occupiers, building workers**

This former railway sidings for the Beckton gasworks had planning permission for 700 homes, see Figure 10.1. Two-thirds of the proposed dwellings were two-storey houses with private gardens. The site is located in East Beckton, south of the A13 trunk road and Beckton Industrial Park. It was contaminated with a variety of materials associated with the coal carbonisation process used in the production of town gas. There is a risk associated with this type of development in that vegetables might be grown in the gardens and contaminants taken up in the plant growth could pass into the food chain. Children could be expected to play in the gardens and may eat the soil, known as Pica Syndrome.

The site was originally part of the East Ham Marshes, as the name implies this was a low lying area drained by natural and man-made channels for agricultural use. In 1868 the site was acquired by the Gas, Coke and Light Company and gas production commenced in 1870. Beckton Gas Works eventually became the largest producer of 'town gas' in the world.

Although the case study area was not part of the main gas production site, there were some storage tanks and gas storage vessels at the extreme eastern edge of the site, all of which were removed prior to redevelopment. The main use of the case study site was the stockpiling of coal, coke and breeze (small cinders, coke dust etc.).

Several chemical and geotechnical site investigations, carried out between 1982 and 1997, were used to arrive at conclusions regarding the levels of contamination during the feasibility study, and as a basis for the site reclamation design. The site investigations found that the made ground on the site was widely contaminated with gas-works related contaminants and those related to coal/coke handling. In many cases the contaminant concentrations exceeded the appropriate trigger and action levels for housing, amenity and/or industrial use. Remediation of the site was therefore required as part of the redevelopment process

The site was developed by a consortium of housing associations to provide 403 houses at affordable rents, with funding from the Housing Corporation and the London Docklands Development Corporation (LDDC), see site layout, Figure 10.2. Funding for a further 63 homes was also secured, together with the funding for two shops and 39 shared ownership houses. Funding was secured from the area health authority for a care in the community scheme. There was also funding for community facilities and a new junior school.

Originally part of a comprehensive proposal for the redevelopment of the Royal Albert Dock, by Rosehaugh Stanhope Developments PLC, the land was acquired by the housing association consortium in March 1990.

Prior to purchase LDDC commissioned a reclamation contract for the site. The land reclamation scheme comprised capping, re-grading and the construction of major site roads and services.

The site remediation involved the formation of a break layer consisting of coarse crushed concrete with zero fines, covered in terram, capped with varying thicknesses of imported materials. The capping layer was designed in such a way as to present a domed section, higher in the centre, so as to allow surface water run-off to the perimeters of the site. The remediation scheme was designed so as to prevent all possible contact between future occupiers and the underlying contamination.

Following concerns expressed by residents about the migration of contamination, consultants were engaged to undertake a further site investigation. This investigation was designed to assess the degree of contamination, if any, present in the surface soil (top 500mm) of the site and to determine the extent, if any, of any upward migration of contaminants, through the break layer and into the capping materials. The potential risk to residents and visitors was to be assessed.

The consultants concluded that there was no evidence to suggest that there is any migration of contaminants upwards through the break layer and into the overlying capping materials. No remedial measures were recommended in relation to the contamination detected within the capping materials, as the concentrations of contaminants were considered to be acceptable for the purpose for which it was intended. In other words, the consultants considered the site to be 'suitable for use' and they commented that the quality of the soil in Winsor Park was generally of better quality, in respect of contamination, than in many areas in other parts of London.

The risk assessment carried out by the consultants used computer modelling, based on the lengthy exposure of children as the most sensitive portion of the population.

Although the risk assessment did not indicate any cause for concern, the consultants recommended that additional tests be carried out at five locations. There was close liaison between the Planning, Environmental Health and Housing departments at the London Borough of Newham, and with the site owner London Docklands Development Corporation which also had the development control powers for the area. The programme involved regular co-ordinating meetings of all relevant officers and the housing association to agree and monitor progress of the scheme.

A management company carries out management of the completed reclamation scheme and is responsible for ongoing monitoring of the contamination situation. The management company holds a sinking fund, secured as part of the land acquisition costs, which currently stands at £4 million. This fund is available if there is any need to undertake work to keep the reclamation scheme in good working order. The sinking fund was required because the undertakings from consultants were not sufficient to secure long-term insurance for the reclamation works.

Work on the site remediation commenced in 1987 and was completed in 1989. The housing association development has now been occupied for eight years. In addition to the East Thames Housing Association development, there were four additional developments undertaken on the land covered by the reclamation scheme. Barratt developed 50 homes for sale on the south-east corner of the site. A self-build scheme of 24 homes was located at the centre of the southern boundary, 30 homes for sale and a 90 bed-space private care home were constructed in the centre of the site. These schemes and the sales of units did not appear to be affected by the site's previous use and reclamation, even though all new purchasers had to become shareholders in the management company. This involved them in having to sign legal agreements that clearly spelt out the nature of the scheme and imposed a legal responsibility to pay service charges to maintain the reclamation works.

Redevelopment of the former gas works complex was still continuing in early 2000, with two private housing developments on parts of the site not covered by the reclamation scheme described above. The first of these, 'Heronhurst' by Barrett East London, comprises 20 freehold houses and 140 apartments in five blocks, sold on 999 year leases. All of the properties are sold with a 10 year NHBC structural warranty.

The second private development, 'Hallywell Place' by Wilcon Homes Eastern, comprises 107 detached, semi-detached and terraced houses. The two and three-bedroom houses all have private rear gardens. The areas to the front are generally used for private parking with a small lawned area. Remediation for this development involved site clearance, removing 40,000 tonnes of contaminated soil, a capillary break layer of crushed stone and the laying of a geo-synthetic clay liner over the landscaped garden areas. This provided a barrier between the subsoil and topsoil of the gardens and any contamination remaining below the break layer.

Comment

Whilst the site remediation method was considered adequate to prepare the site for the housing association redevelopment, it did not allay the fears of the residents.

More than one form of remediation, or site preparation technique may be employed on the same site and the choice of method used may change over time.

KEY POINTS

- When planning a site investigation consideration should be given to the need to relate the investigation to the requirements of an insurance company, in case it is decided to seek cover for remediation cost over-run insurance or in respect of the remediation itself.

- It may be necessary to establish a sinking fund, administrated by a management company, if future maintenance work is likely to be required or if insurance cover is not available.

DETR Industry Profiles: Gas works, coke works and other coal carbonisation plants; Railway land

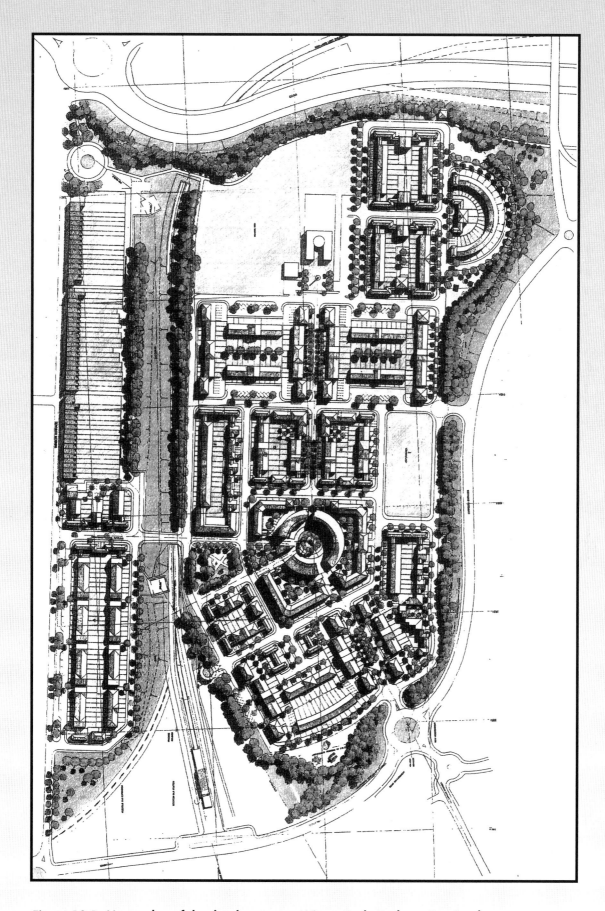

Figure 10.1 Masterplan of the development at Winsor Park, Beckton, East London

11. Road haulage

- EXCAVATION AND OFF-SITE DISPOSAL
- PRIVATE FOR SALE AND ELDERLY PERSONS BUNGALOWS

Location:	**Rothwell, Leeds**
Size of site:	**2.79 hectares**
Contaminants:	**arsenic and gas works wastes**
Potential receptors:	**occupiers and building workers**

This scheme involves the development of 67 homes by Alfred McAlpine on a site near Rothwell Park, Leeds. Included as part of the development scheme were nine social housing bungalows for the elderly, situated close to the town centre edge of the site. This satisfied a planning requirement imposed by Leeds City Council. The private sector dwellings comprised two and three bedroom semi-detached housing for sale.

The site was formerly occupied by a road haulage firm and no other previous use had been recorded at the site. The site had been identified as an area of general industry in the Leeds UDP. Alfred McAlpine purchased the site subject to a site investigation.

The site investigation and remediation strategy was undertaken by AIG Consultants, consisting of 21 trial pits and 31 bore holes, and a total of 17 samples were analysed. The concentration levels for metals and metalloids were compared against ICRCL levels for domestic gardens and allotments. Following this, a supplementary investigation of 15 trial pits was undertaken to obtain additional information.

Three of the samples tested, made ground from Trial Pits 2, 3 and 4, were viewed as comprising of or containing a gas works-derived waste, comprising tarry ash with occasional spent oxide fragments (this probably originated from a nearby town gas works). The 'gas works' origin of the waste was confirmed by extremely high results obtained for total petroleum hydrocarbon, toluene extractable matter, zinc, cyanide and sulphate.

Two other samples of made ground, in Trial Pits 10 and 12, also showed a high level of petroleum hydrocarbons and toluene extractable matter. They also showed slightly elevated arsenic levels. Two narrow bands of bituminous gravel were encountered in TP10 and were considered to be the source of high organic contamination. A total sulphate concentration of 4,320mg/kg found in the sample of made ground in TP11 exceeded the threshold level but was well below the action level. It was therefore considered by the environmental consultant that sulphate levels did not constitute a risk on this site. Arsenic exceeded the ICRCL threshold level of 10mg/kg in seven of the samples tested with a maximum of 38.9mg/kg in TP3 at 0.50m below ground level.

Boron was the only phytotoxic element to be detected in a sample not identified as gas works waste. This was found in BH9 in a sample of made ground containing burnt shale. There were no contaminants above respective trigger levels in samples of natural ground.

The site was split into four areas, (A - D), see Figure 11.1. Area A adjoins onto green-belt land and was uncontaminated, Area B runs along the back edge and previously had a hardcore cover on it, Area C, the middle section, had a tarmac cover and the front section (Area D) was covered by concrete slab from former buildings. Area D was the area of particular concern (approx 1400m^2).

Leaving the material from Area D on site was not considered to be a realistic solution. It would have required capping by at least 1m of inert material over a 300mm capillary break layer and then would cause problems during subsequent development when excavations for foundations/services would re-expose contaminated material. There was a slight possibility (although it was not recommended) that the material derived from the gas works waste could be relocated on site in an area of public open space under a suitable depth of cover (Min 1m). It was also considered that due to the nature of the waste that regulatory approval would not be granted for such an option. The consultant's strategy was to recommend all the contaminated material from Area D to be removed from site to a licensed landfill. The removal of this material required the prior notice of the Environment Agency as it was classified as "special waste".

Approximately 2,300m^3 of material was removed during a period of six weeks. The costs of reclamation represented approximately 10% of the total site costs. During this period stringent Health and Safety Measures were required, including:

• full demarcation of the contaminated area with restricted access

• on-site washing facilities

• lorries removing contaminated material off site to be fully sheeted

• waste to be mixed with limestone dust prior to sheeting

The lime stone dust:

• maintains alkaline conditions in the waste

• reacts with soluble sulphate to produce gypsum

- inhibits and attenuates leachate of metallic contaminants and assists in the saponification[5] of phenol contaminants

- "stiffens up" free coal tar

Following removal of the gas works waste, the only remaining contaminants were elevated arsenic concentrations (between 11.1 and 26.2 mg/kg) in five samples of made ground and one elevated boron result. Odours of hydrocarbon were noticed in TP5 during trial pitting although subsequent analysis indicated that the concentrations were below ICRCL trigger levels. Two underground oil interceptors, which did not smell of hydrocarbons, were present on site and were removed.

Due to the fact that some mild contamination was to be left in-situ it was recommended that precautions were required for the concrete used underground in accordance with Class 2 (BRE Digest 363).

There were few issues in relation to the brownfield element of the site that caused any problems with the regulators. The developer did express concerns regarding some of the planning requirements in relation to a S.106 agreement made under the provisions of the Town & Country Planning Act 1990 and indecisiveness between local authority departments. One of the requirements was that 10% of the site should be allocated for extra open space even though it was situated adjacent to a large park. Also one of the conditions stated that trees should be planted in a10 m wide strip along the edge of the green-belt to soften the development, even though the edge of the site backed onto woods.

The development was completed in December 1999 and Alfred McAlpine marketed the homes using an in-house sales team. Sales documentation informed purchasers of the previous use of the site. An A4 sheet was provided with legal documents stating what has been done and what purchasers can expect.

Comment

Given the former use of the site and that there had been no other recorded uses on the site the discovery of gas works related material was unexpected. In this particular case, because of the nature of the waste there was little option but to remove the material from site. However if the contaminated material fell below threshold levels for Public Open Space then that may have reduced costs. Such strategies should be negotiated with regulators before remedial works commence.

---

[5] *Converting it into a 'soap like' substance*

KEY POINTS

- Undertake a comprehensive desk study, preferably prior to purchase of the site.

- If possible talk to previous owners/tenants as they may be able to identify areas of unexpected waste material.

- Identify possible means of leaving material on site.

- Where gas works material is encountered a special wastes certificate will be required and the Environment Agency will need to be informed.

- Where certain contaminants are to be left in-situ special precautions may need to be taken on building structures and services.

DETR Industry Profiles: Road vehicle fuelling, service and repair: transport and haulage centres; Gas works, coke works and other coal carbonisation plants.

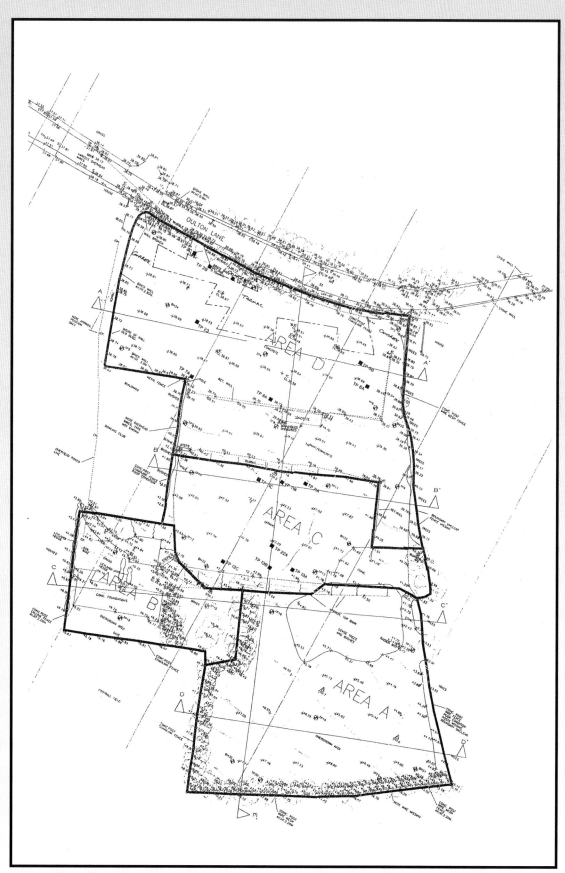

Figure 11.1 Site at Rothwell near Leeds, showing sub-division into four areas for the remediation strategy, together with borehole and trial pit locations

12. Shipbuilding works

- PARTIAL OFF-SITE DISPOSAL, PARTIAL ON-SITE DISPOSAL AND DILUTION
- HOUSING ASSOCIATION RENTED AND SHARED OWNERSHIP, PRIVATE HOUSING FOR SALE, PLUS COMMERCIAL USE AND OPEN SPACE.

Location:	Spencer Street / Navigation Road, Northwich, Cheshire.
Size of site:	3.2 hectares, of which 1.94 hectares developable
Contaminants:	heavy metals
Potential receptors:	ground water, occupiers, building workers

This was a development by Vale Royal Borough Council, in partnership with Lovell Partnerships and Muir Housing Association. The objective of the development was to provide low cost housing for sale, housing for rent and shared ownership.

The site was acquired by Vale Royal Borough Council, for a nominal sum, in 1985 and 1986 from a major chemical company. It was known that contamination may be present from the previous use of the site as a ship building and repair yard.

The original idea was to redevelop the site with much needed council housing and to 'clean up' the site using Derelict Land Grant. However the DLG application was not approved and funding for local authority housing was discontinued.

Two limited scope site investigations were undertaken by consultants appointed by the Council. A risk assessment was carried out by AEA Technology, followed by a third investigation in 1995, to 'fill in the gaps' in the two previous studies.

The site is situated approximately half a mile from Northwich town centre and it is divided into two parts by a railway viaduct, a listed structure, which is still in use, see Figure 12.1. The viaduct is owned by Railtrack and its engineers had to be consulted in respect of any works in the vicinity of the structure. Work on site was further complicated by the presence of sewers and brine mains associated with the local salt mining industry.

The site adjoins the Weaver Navigation and is underlain by boulder clay (with sand and gravel layers and lenses) and the bedrock consists of Lower Keuper Saliferous Beds. Alluvium associated with the flood plain of the River Weaver covers the boulder clay on the eastern two-thirds of the site.

The original topography probably consisted of a steep slope down from Spencer Street, with a flat plain extending to the River Weaver. When the Weaver Navigation cut was made, the excavated spoil was probably dumped close by and what is described as alluvium may consist of undisturbed alluvial deposits covered by this excavated material.

The site investigations revealed that much of the site area was covered by fill materials, possibly including household waste, demolition material and waste products from the former shipyard. Anecdotal evidence, provided by a local resident during the course of the AEA Technology site investigation, suggested that quantities of asbestos had been tipped on part of the site. The area indicated was carefully investigated but no significant concentrations of asbestos were found.

Groundwater entries were inconsistent, with water entries being recorded in both the fill and the alluvium and, occasionally, in the sand within the boulder clay. This indicated the presence of perched water in several locations across the site and there was also the possibility of continuity with water in the adjoining Weaver Navigation.

AEA Technology concluded that remedial action was required if the site was to be redeveloped for housing use. Two remediation options were considered, namely:

(a) excavation and removal of all soil for off-site disposal; and

(b) classification of the contaminated material for off-site disposal and/or re-use on site.

The second option was selected as the first was uneconomic and would have caused considerable disruption to the local traffic system.

The contaminated material was classified into three categories, as follows:

Category 1: Material with contaminant concentrations above ICRCL threshold or action levels for public open space and/or metals that are leachable;

Category 2: Material below ICRCL trigger levels for public open space but above ICRCL trigger values for domestic gardens and allotments. Metals which are non-leachable.

Category 3: Material below ICRCL trigger values for domestic gardens and allotments including non-leachable metals.

The category 1 material was further divided into two sub-categories, with only material containing leachable metals being removed from site (a provision was made for the removal of up to 2,000 tonnes) for disposal to a licensed landfill. The remaining category 1 material was deposited into a proposed public open space area in the southern part of the site, beyond the railway viaduct. Up to 21,000 tonnes of category 2 material was also removed to this area. The earthworks in the public open space were designed to act as a flood protection barrier.

Remaining category 2 material and category 3 material was retained within the northern part of the site, the development area, and used to raise the ground level adjacent to the River. All material deposited in the public open space area, landscaping areas within the development and the domestic gardens were covered with a clay and topsoil cap.

Having carried out the site investigations and decided upon a remediation strategy, Vale Royal Borough Council prepared a development brief which was sent to several housing developers known to be active in the area. A mix of tenures was to be provided and the housing for sale was to be priced at the lower end of the market. The development brief stipulated that approximately one third of the site was to be made available for housing association development, thereby satisfying the Council's immediate need for social housing.

Part of the development was to include commercial buildings, in the north-eastern corner of the site, behind some existing industrial units. These uses complied with the local plan.

Interested developers had to submit their proposals, with a development layout and illustrative elevations. Following this, interviews were held by a members and officers working group of the Council, which resulted in Lovell Partnerships and Muir Housing Association being appointed as the development partners. Lovell Partnerships is a very experienced housing developer with a long history of undertaking partnership projects with local authorities and housing associations. The company undertook its own demand study and concluded that it was possible to integrate the social and shared ownership housing units with the 'housing for sale' development - i.e. not separating the different tenures into discrete areas of the site.

The architect appointed by Lovell Partnerships worked up the development proposal and submitted the planning application. The site remediation strategy was submitted as part of the planning application and the planning permission was conditioned to the effect that work on the development should not commence until such time as the scheme of remediation had been implemented.

As part of the planning process a public exhibition was held to explain the development proposals to local residents. Whilst the Council considered the site to be a contaminated eyesore, over 300 local residents attended the public meeting and it was clear, from the views expressed, that they enjoyed the use of the land as an amenity area. Dogs were exercised on the derelict site and children used it as a play area.

The Council contributed the land to the development at nil cost but, even with this, the development was not economically viable due to the high cost of site remediation. An application was made to English Partnerships for gap funding, so as to enable the project to proceed. At first this application was not well received as Northwich was not in a priority area for EP investment funding but, eventually, approval was given for a grant of £545,750 against project expenditure of £3,750,000.

Work commenced in April 1998 and the housing development was completed in September 1999. Site remediation work was undertaken during April and May 1998. Although the site was not totally remediated, as some contaminated material was retained on site, the work was undertaken to the satisfaction of the Council's Environmental Health Department and the Environment Agency. The remediation work was undertaken by a sub-contractor to Lovell Partnerships, with AEA Technology supervising the work by way of periodic visits to the site. AEA Technology then prepared a completion report describing the work that had been undertaken.

Before work commenced it was brought to the attention of the development team that part of the open space area in the southern part of the site was a locally important wetland. Therefore this area had to be protected and could not be tipped with contaminated spoil. The railway viaduct presented a further constraint on the development proposals, in that houses built too close to this listed structure could be undesirable, due to the over-powering height of the viaduct.

The commercial development has not yet been carried out but there are plans for this to be developed as an environment centre, as a partnership between VRBC and Groundwork Trust (Macclesfield and Vale Royal).

As a result of the experience gained from dealing with this site, Vale Royal Borough Council has established a 'development team approach' to deal with future development proposals involving contaminated land, comprising representatives from planning, building control and environmental health. Intending developers are encouraged to contact the team at the earliest possible opportunity.

Comment

A derelict site is not necessarily perceived by everyone to be an eyesore, even if it is contaminated, and it is important to involve the local community at an early stage of the project.

Key points

- Local knowledge is important with regard to past uses and possible deposits of contamination.

- Even if the land is made available for redevelopment at nil cost the redevelopment project still may not be viable and grant aid may be needed.

- It was not necessary to remove all of the contamination from the site, the contaminant pathway was broken or removed instead.

DETR Industry Profiles: Engineering works: Shipbuilding, repair and ship-breaking.

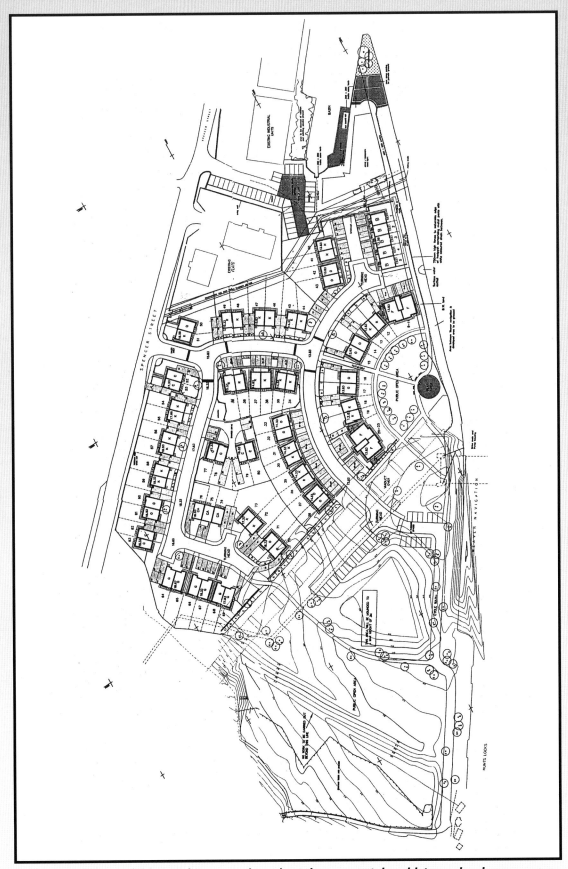

Figure 12.1 Successful layout for a mixed residential, commercial and leisure development at Northwich, Cheshire

13. Timber mill

- EXCAVATION AND OFF-SITE DISPOSAL/ COVER & CONTAIN
- HOUSING ASSOCIATION, SHARED OWNERSHIP

Location: Walkergate, Newcastle upon Tyne
Size of site: 0.53 hectares
Contaminants: heavy metals, polycyclic aromatic hydrocarbons, sulphates
Potential receptors: occupiers, building workers

Construction work has recently started on the site of a former timber yard and sawmill. The site is being developed for 13 detached and semi-detached bungalows, built for Home Housing Association by Leech Homes Ltd. They will be offered to the elderly for shared ownership. The site was owned by Newcastle City Council and became available due to the expiry of a 60 year lease. The City Council was willing to see a change of use to housing, given that there was an acute need of homes for elderly persons in the area, for which Home Housing Association had an allocation.

The site is roughly triangular in shape with the rear fence line forming the eastern boundary. To the west is a nursery school and the south and south west of the site bounds onto playing fields. The site is fairly compact and access is shared with the nursery school, see Figure 13.1.

There was an area of made ground which was presumed to be infilling of a former valley towards the south of the site. Historic records also indicated that several coal seams have been worked below the site at depths in the region of 200m below ground level.

The timber yard was the only previous known use that had occupied the site. Prior to redevelopment the structures included a timber saw mill, two storey sandstone house and a range of timber and corrugated iron outbuildings. Due to vandalism these buildings were demolished before the site was sold. Site observations indicated a small timber treatment plant in the southern part of the site with railway lines running to/from this building. There were a number of semi-mature and mature deciduous trees along the northern and western site boundaries.

Geological records indicate the site to be underlain by boulder clay overlying a sandstone of the Middle Coal Measures. Environment Agency information indicated the boulder clay and Middle Coal Measures to be minor aquifers.

Home Housing Association always undertakes a full site investigation before buying a site and, on the instruction of Leech Homes Ltd. (the developer appointed by the housing association), consultants WSP Environmental Ltd were appointed to undertake a site investigation and prepare a suitable remediation method statement. A phased investigation was undertaken in February 1999, comprising:

- 5 No cable percussion boreholes

- chemical analysis (7 samples for a range of contaminants, in accordance with ICRCL guidance) on samples from the boreholes

- leachate analysis

- pesticide screening (3 samples)

- a number of hand excavated trial holes

- chemical analysis (20 samples) for arsenic, cadmium, copper, nickel, zinc, boron, phenol and Polycyclic Aromatic Hydrocarbons (PAH)

- gas monitoring

The site investigation boreholes recorded made ground, generally composed of black ash and brick fragments at depths between 0.8m and 1.60m below ground level. In all locations the made ground was underlain by a stiff and very stiff sandy silty clay. No groundwater was encountered during the site investigation

The initial seven soil samples were analysed for a range of common contaminants as defined in relevant ICRCL guidance notes. The results were all compared with the relevant threshold trigger concentrations for 'residential' end uses. Concentrations of arsenic, cadmium, boron, copper, nickel, zinc, phenols, PAH and total sulphate were all recorded in excess of the threshold trigger level.

A further twenty soil samples recorded widespread contamination, the results of which are shown below in Table 13.1:

Table 13.1 Soil samples exceeding Threshold Trigger Concentrations*

	Number of samples exceeding TTC*	Range of contaminant concentrations mg/kg	
		Min	Max
Arsenic	23	4.6	29.8
Cadmium	4	<2.0	5.5
Copper	12	22	811
Nickel	4	21	130
Zinc	18	52	3490
Boron	2	1.05	15
Phenol	14 (2)	<1.5	1520
PAH	18 (8)	6.8	4400

Values in brackets relate to Action trigger levels

Source: WSP Environmental, 1999

Discussions between the environmental consultant and the former tenant of the property indicated that timber treatment was made using a non-toxic and non-flammable water based material (Protocol Fenocote). Analysis for organo-chlorine compounds, typically used in wood treatment failed to find any concentrations above analytical detection limits. Leachate analyses indicated the potential for leaching of contaminants to be low. No groundwater was encountered during the investigation and the site is underlain by at least 5m of low permeability boulder clay. It was therefore considered that the site did not pose a significant risk to groundwater.

Landfill gas readings were obtained from standpipes installed in two boreholes. The monitoring recorded no methane present and carbon dioxide concentrations of 1.1% and 1.6%. The consultants recommended no special precautions in relation to landfill gas, but suggested that, where suspended floors were to be used, provision be made for sub-floor ventilation.

On the basis of the initial results the consultants recommended that the contaminated soils identified close to the railway lines and around the former timber treatment bath be removed from site for disposal to landfill. They stressed that care should be taken during site clearance in order to prevent further spillages of timber preservative. All areas of hydrocarbon contamination, identified from the site investigation, needed to be clearly marked on site and all materials within these areas had to be bagged or drummed for disposal to a suitably licensed waste disposal site. This material was classified as special waste.

The remediation works were supervised by a qualified resident engineer in accordance with NHBC Standards, Chapter 4.1. Land Quality - managing ground conditions.

Trees were an issue on this site due to the fact that the city council wished to see as many preserved as possible. If all contamination were to be removed from site it would have meant removing all of the trees. This was unacceptable to the city council and it was agreed to leave material under the tree roots along the perimeter of the site and additional landscaping was required, as shown on Figure 13.1.

The final remediation strategy for the scheme minimised the off-site disposal of material by removing contaminated soil from rear gardens only and importing clean clay and top soil to a depth of 0.5m. Where deep foundations had been used some of the less contaminated material was placed under the houses. The front gardens were hard landscaped to remove the possibility of residents accessing the soil underneath. This was a compromise between the developer and the city council which had wished to see some form of break layer used. Monitoring of the site remediation work was carried out by the developer under a design and build contract.

It is not intended to provide specific information relating to the history of the site and its remediation but copies of the decontamination certificate will be provided to purchasers' solicitors upon completion of the development.

Comment

This study highlights the difficulties faced by both developer and regulator. This was only a small development and a cost effective remediation strategy was required. Due to the design and build nature of the contract the developer had to examine alternative design layouts so that the off-site disposal of contaminated material could be minimised. The City Council could have enforced a break layer which would have increased the cost of the development and therefore made it unprofitable. The retention of trees and the close proximity to the nursery school also provided a problem for which a compromise solution was needed.

KEY POINTS

* Examine the layout of the site and identify alternative remediation strategies given different design layouts.

* Liaise with former owners/tenants to identify any chemicals that may have been used on site.

* Different local authorities may have alternative views of how to deal with a site. Discussions with them at an early stage may save unnecessary complications later in the development.

DETR Industry Profile: Timber treatment works

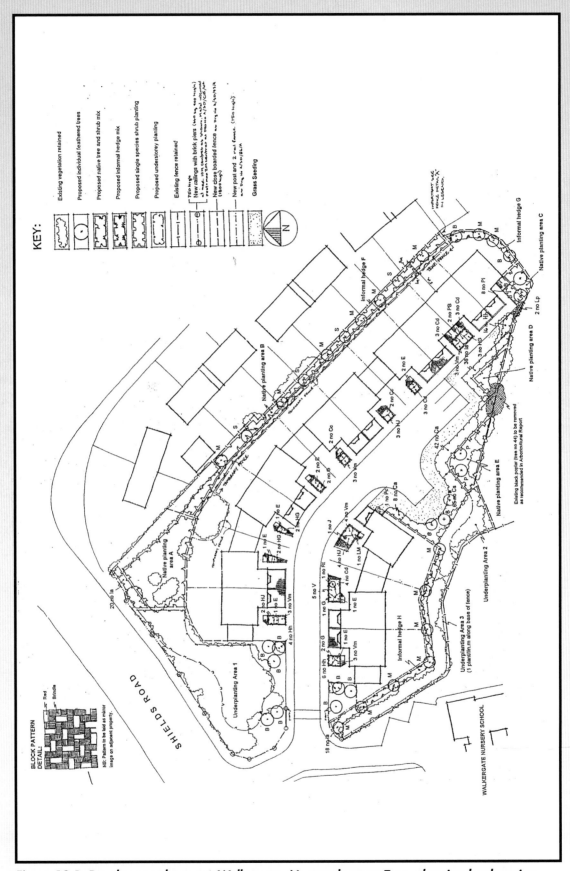

Figure 13.1 Development layout at Walkergate, Newcastle-upon-Tyne, showing landscaping reinforcement to retain trees following decontamination of site

14. Recommendations for the redevelopment of previously used land

When the research for this case studies report commenced, it did so with a very positive attitude towards the redevelopment of previously used and contaminated land. It was not the intention, or the authors' remit, to criticise housing developers or to castigate regulatory authorities. Equally, the objective was not to make recommendations as to future policies for either Government or the house building industry. Instead, as part of the Joseph Rowntree Foundation 'policies into practice' programme, the objective was to investigate how different builders, regulatory authorities, consultants and other actors approached the problems of site redevelopment.

A number of very important conclusions can be drawn from the case studies, not least that every site is unique and intending developers, their consultants and regulatory authorities need to be aware that the solution adopted in one situation may be totally unsuitable in another. The conclusions lead into a series of recommendations that have been grouped according to the eleven phases of redevelopment identified in chapter one.

Project inception - developers and regulators must be prepared to act in a flexible manner to achieve the redevelopment of 'previously used' or 'brownfield' land and buildings. This may entail changing the type of scheme to be developed and 'what if' alternatives need to be reflected in the development appraisals. It is possible that sites identified for residential development in local plans or Unitary Development Plans are in fact unsuited to that type of use, due to contamination or other problems in the ground.

Site acquisition and site assembly - landowners may have completely unrealistic ideas about the value of their land but, equally, they may be trapped by historic valuations and the fact that the land is used as collateral against bank borrowings or other loans. Letters of intent, options and conditional contracts must be carefully worded, clearly identifying who is to do what and who will be responsible for bearing what proportion of the costs.

Site assessment - it is important to identify any access or site constraints, including the adequacy of infrastructure, which may affect the development. All site assessments must initially comprise of an historical study followed by a 'walkover' survey. It some cases it will be necessary for intrusive investigations to be undertaken in several stages, developing the site assessment in the light of knowledge obtained from the earlier work. Whilst it may be desirable to obtain a 'fixed price' quotation from the environmental consultant, this may not always be possible, especially if the extent of laboratory testing cannot be determined at the outset. If possible talk to previous owners, tenants and local residents, as they may be able to assist in locating unexpected deposits of waste material.

Contaminant-pathway-receptor - all possible linkages should be considered. Remember that it may not be necessary to remove all contamination from the site, it may be feasible to break or remove the pathway instead. This option must, however, be considered in the context of how it is likely to be viewed by future house buyers or tenants.

Detailed design - examine the layout of the site and be prepared to consider alternative remediation strategies given different layouts. On sites affected by landfill gas, address the gas protection, venting and monitoring measures at an early stage, as part of the integrated design process. If monitoring is required, then the development will probably be most suited for 'managed' (usually rented) housing. Agree in advance the duration of any monitoring, or the criteria to be achieved before monitoring is discontinued. Remember different local authorities may have different ideas in respect of monitoring, often driven by their previous experience.

Feasibility study - having completed the site assessment and having identified all potential pollutant linkages, the revised design should be the subject of a comprehensive review. It is possible that a considerable period of time, at least several months and possibly more than a year, will have elapsed since the project inception phase and it may be advisable to undertake a new demand study, especially if the nature of the development proposal has undergone any significant changes.

Planning and regulatory approvals - close liaison with the regulators during the earlier phases should ensure that the necessary information has been collected and can be presented in support of the applications. The ways in which existing planning guidance on contaminated land is applied does vary between authorities but it is important, from the developer's point of view, to ensure that all relevant information is available and is fully understood by the regulators. The need, or otherwise, for Waste Management or Mobile Plant licences should be identified as early as possible.

Development finance - banks and other financial institutions are probably more prepared to provide development finance for 'previously used' sites than they were a few years ago, but there are still a few exceptions. Financiers will, almost certainly, require full site investigation reports and may insist on appointing their own environmental consultants to comment upon the reports. They may also wish to oversee the remediation works. There may be some reluctance to provide finance for projects that involve innovative, or relatively untried, remediation methodologies. Possible sources of grant aid should be identified and negotiations commenced as soon as possible after project inception. Remember, even if the land is included at nil cost the project may still not be viable without some public sector support.

Tendering - the appointment of contractors with experience of site remediation can be beneficial, as they may be able to suggest ways of undertaking the work. The tendering process will, inevitably, vary with some developers having established relationships with contractors, leading to a negotiated contract, whilst others will undertake a full competitive tendering process. Either way, the scope of the work should be adequately described but it is not the task of this report to discuss the 'pros and cons' of design and build versus traditional contracts.

Construction - the site remediation/preparation works must be properly supervised and, most importantly, must be fully recorded - ideally this will involve maintaining photographic and written records, including sketches of where contaminants, or other site constraints such as old services, were located. Remember, debris from previous uses, including glass, metal and plastics, can be just as harmful to small children as chemical contaminants and should be removed as part of the remediation contract.

Sales and marketing - this includes the communication of information, to prospective purchasers and tenants, as to the previous use of the site, the contaminants found and the methods employed to prepare the site for redevelopment. Developers will have different ways of dealing with this. Some will be quite open about the site history, including 'before' photographs in the sales office and on brochures, whereas others will only provide information as part of the package sent to purchasers' solicitors. Either way, it is important to be open with information relating to the site and its development, as any attempt at concealment is likely to have an adverse effect once it is discovered.

Developers need to be aware of the fact that the lists of potentially contaminative industrial uses provided in publications such as the DETR Industry Profiles and the RICS 'Red Book' Guidance Note 2 are not exhaustive. Uses such as school laboratories, hospitals and research centres may cause contamination. It should never be assumed that a site is 'clean', even agricultural activities can result in contamination, from leaking fuel storage tanks to the use of pesticides and insecticides.

In undertaking this research, it became clear that in most cases 'stigma' was not the issue the media would have us believe. Most of the developers contacted during the course of the research were committed to the redevelopment of brownfield sites, and many had extensive knowledge and experience. With the support of the regulatory authorities in guiding the re-use of land, there should be no reason not to redevelop all but the most severely contaminated sites. Whether or not all sites would make a 'pleasant place to live' is another issue. Communication between developer and occupier is one of the most important factors in ensuring a successful development.

References and source material

Acer Consultants Ltd., (1995) 'Reclamation Strategy, Leicester City Challenge, Bede Island North, Leicester', unpublished report.

AEA Technology, (1999) 'Remedial Validation Report, Spencer Street, Northwich', unpublished report.

AIG Consultants, (1996) 'Land at Oulton Lane, Rothwell: Geotechnical and Contamination Appraisal', unpublished report.

Ashton, J (2000) 'Wimpey wishes for housing slowdown', Daily Telegraph, London, 23 February 2000, 1734.

Baker, B. (2000) 'The Safe Development of Housing on Land Affected by Contamination', paper presented at a Construction Industry Environmental Forum meeting, 11th May, 2000.

Clayton Environmental Consultants Ltd., (1994) 'Soil Quality Assurance Programme, Sampling, Analysis and Risk Assessment: Winsor Park, Beckton', unpublished report.

Construction Industry Research and Information Association (CIRIA) - 'Remedial Treatment for Contaminated Land, in 12 volumes - volume III (1995) *Site investigation and assessment*, volume IV (1995) *Classification and selection of remedial methods*, CIRIA, London.

Department of the Environment (DETR), (1994) *Guidance on Preliminary Site inspection of Contaminated Land*, a Contaminated Land Research Report (CLR 2) prepared by Applied Environmental Research Centre Ltd., Department of the Environment, London (2 volumes).

Department of the Environment, (1994) *Documentary Research on Industrial Sites*, a Contaminated Land Research Report (CLR 3) prepared by RPS Consultants Ltd., Department of the Environment, London.

Department of the Environment, (1994) *Sampling Strategies for Contaminated Land*, a Contaminated Land Research Report (CLR4) prepared by The Centre for Research into the Built Environment, Nottingham Trent University, Department of the Environment, London.

Department of the Environment, (1996) *Household Growth: where shall we live?* a green paper Cm 3471, The Stationery Office, London.

Department of the Environment, (2000) *Planning Policy Guidance Note 3: Housing* (PPG3), The Stationery Office, London.

Environmental Protection Act 1990, HMSO, London.

Environment Act 1995, HMSO, London.

Hyder (1999) 'Reclamation Strategy - Site A1 Anchor Road, Grahams Yard and Brandon Shed, Bristol', unpublished report.

Housing Corporation, The (1998) *Scheme Development Standards*, The Housing Corporation, London.

Interdepartmental Committee on the Redevelopment of Contaminated Land (ICRCL), (1987) *Guidance on the assessment and redevelopment of contaminated land*, guidance note 59/83, second edition, ICRCL, London.

Kelly, R. (1999) ' A brown and unpleasant land', *The Times*, London, 23 January.

Komex, Clarke Bond (1997) 'Desk Study and interpretative report', Busby's Garage, Milton Street, Fairford, unpublished report.

Komex, Clarke Bond (1998) 'Environmental assessment and interpretative report', Busby's Garage, Milton Street, Fairford, unpublished report.

Komex (1999) 'Validation report for remedial works, Busby's Garage, Milton Street, Fairford', unpublished report.

Martin I. & Bardos P., (1995) *A Review of Full Scale Treatment technologies for the Remediation of Contaminated Soil*, EPP Publications, Richmond.

National House-Building Council (1999) Standards Chapter 4.1 'Land Quality - managing ground conditions', NHBC, Amersham.

Parliamentary Office of Science and Technology (POST) (1998), *A Brown and Pleasant Land: household growth and brownfield sites*, Report 117, POST, London.

Perowne, M (1998) 'Factories need homes as well', Viewpoint in *Estates Gazette*, 16th May, 9820, 34.

Salford City Council, (1997) 'Douglas Green/ Whit Lane Area: Development Opportunity', development brief, Civic Centre, Salford.

Sherritt, B. (2000) 'Designing Construction Projects on Brownfield Sites - a consultant's point of view', presentation to a Construction Industry Environmental Forum meeting 11th May, 2000.

Simkins, E. (1997) 'Fear over greenfield housing', *Estates Gazette*, London, 8 November.

Syms, P.M. (1995) 'Piccadilly Village, Manchester: a case study in waterside urban renewal' in Urban Renewal, Berry J., S. McGreal and B. Deddis (eds), E&FN Spon, London.

Syms, P.M. (1997) *The Redevelopment of Contaminated Land for Housing Use*, ISVA (now Royal Institution of Chartered Surveyors), London.

Syms, P.M. (1999) *Desk Reference Guide to potentially Contaminative Land Uses*, ISVA (now Royal Institution of Chartered Surveyors), London.

Syms, P.M. (2000) *Releasing Brownfields*, a research report funded by the Joseph Rowntree Foundation, forthcoming, Autumn.

Urban Task Force (1999), *Towards an Urban Renaissance*, E & FN Spon, London.

Vale Royal Borough Council, (1994) 'Development Brief for Land at Spencer Street/Navigation Road, Northwich, Cheshire', unpublished.

Welsh Development Agency (1993) *The WDA Manual on the Remediation of Contaminated Land*, prepared by ECOTEC Research & Consulting and Environmental Advisory Unit, WDA, Cardiff.

Wilkinson Architects, Chris. (1991) 'Winsor Park Housing East Beckton London E6', a report prepared for National Housing Week.

WSP Environmental Ltd., (1999) Remediation Method Statement, Walkergate, Shields Road, Newcastle-upon-Tyne, unpublished report.

Appendix 1: The 'contaminated land legislation'

Part IIA of the Environmental Protection Act 1990 was brought into being by way of section 57 of the Environment Act 1995 and became effective in April 2000. The legislation provides a statutory definition of **'contaminated land'** as being

any land which appears to the local authority in whose area it is situated to be in such a condition, by reason of substances in, on or under the land, that-

(a) significant harm is being caused or there is a significant possibility of such harm being caused; or

(b) pollution of controlled waters is being, or is likely to be, caused;

The primary regulators under the legislation are the local authorities, and they are placed under a duty to inspect their areas for the purposes of identifying and bringing about the remediation of land determined to be contaminated in accordance with this definition. Commencing in April 2000 the authorities were given a period of fifteen months to prepare their strategies for implementation of the legislation.

In order that land may be determined as being contaminated in accordance with the legislation, it is necessary for the regulator to identify at least one **'significant pollutant linkage'**, whereby a **'contaminant'** can travel, or be transmitted via a **'pathway'** to a **'receptor'**, or target. There are four receptor groups, human beings, protected ecological environments (e.g. Sites of Special Scientific Interest), domestic animals and crops, and buildings. The extent to which 'harm' may be deemed 'significant' for possible receptors in each group is given in statutory guidance issued by the Department of Environment, Transport and the Regions - see www.environment.detr.gov.uk.

Regulatory authorities have the power to require **'appropriate persons'** to take action to remediate land identified as being contaminated, either through voluntary action or through the use of **'Remediation notices'**. The degree of remediation required under the legislation is no more than would be necessary to render the land **'suitable for use'** and to prevent risks to human health or the environment in relation to the current use or a future use of the land for which planning permission is being sought. In this context the term **'remediation'** includes site investigation.

Having determined that a site is contaminated in accordance with the statutory definition, the regulator then has to identify the **'appropriate person'** or persons to bear all, or part, of the remediation cost. This is done using the **'polluter pays'** principle but, if the polluter cannot be found, or no longer exists, the responsibility falls to the current landowner, defined as being the person entitled to receive the rack rent. There are provisions for **'hardship'**, which may protect the innocent landowner from having to meet all, or even any, of the cost, in which case the regulator becomes liable for the remediation.

In situations where there is more than one possible **'appropriate person'** and in order to decide who should bear what proportion of the cost, the regulator has to apply six exclusion tests. The parties are divided into two **'Liability Classes'** - Class A comprising all possible polluters and Class B the landowners. The exclusion tests are then applied to the Class A persons:-

TEST 1 - "EXCLUDED ACTIVITIES"

Persons whose only involvement has been in respect of the following will, normally, be excluded from liability:

(a) providing (or withholding) financial assistance, such as a loan, grant, guarantee or indemnity;

(b) underwriting an insurance policy under which another person was insured and where that person might be held to have knowingly permitted the pollution to have occurred;

(c) carrying out any action for the purpose of assessing whether or not to provide financial assistance or to underwrite an insurance policy;

(d) consigning, as waste, to another person the substance comprising the significant pollutant, under a contract whereby that person knowingly took over responsibility for its proper disposal or other management;

(e) creating a tenancy over the land in favour of another person who has caused or knowingly permitted the contamination;

(f) as an owner creating a licence over the land, except where the person granting the licence operated the site for the disposal or storage of waste at the time the licence was granted;

(g) issuing any statutory permission, licence or consent;

(h) taking, or not taking, any statutory enforcement action in respect of the land or against some other person;

(i) providing legal, financial, engineering, scientific or technical advice in respect of the land;

(j) as a person providing services described in (i), carrying out any intrusive investigation, except where the investigation creates the significant pollutant linkage and the client is not a member of the liability group;

(k) performing any contract by providing a service or by supplying goods, where the contract is made with another person who is also a member of the liability group in question.

TEST 2 - "PAYMENTS MADE FOR REMEDIATION"

This is intended to exclude from liability persons who have already recognised their responsibilities by making a payment to another member of the liability group for the purpose of ensuring remediation of the site. The payment, at the time it was made, must have been sufficient to pay for the remediation in question but the remediation was either not done or was not carried out effectively. If, however, the person making the payment retains any control over the condition of the land, after the date of payment, then this test does not apply.

TEST 3 - "SOLD WITH INFORMATION"

The intention here is to exclude from liability persons, polluters, who have sold the land and, at the time of sale, have provided the buyer with information as to the presence on the land of the pollutant identified in the significant pollutant linkage. This may occur where a developer acquires land for redevelopment and accepts responsibility for remediation. The sale may involve both a reduction in price (Test 2) and the supply of information by the vendor. For the vendor to be excluded from liability the sale has to be at arms' length and the vendor must not retain any interest in, or any right to use or occupy the land.

TEST 4 - "CHANGES TO SUBSTANCES"

The purpose here is to exclude from liability persons who deposited a substance on or in the land which, in itself, did not constitute a pollutant to the extent that it would be likely to cause significant harm or pollution of controlled waters. However, through the actions or omissions of another person, or persons, another substance has been introduced at a later date, causing the original substance to change its characteristics, by chemical reaction, biological process or some other change, to the extent that it has become a **'significant pollutant'**. For the first party to be excluded from liability it is necessary to demonstrate that the earlier substance would not have formed part of the **'significant**

pollutant linkage' if the change had not taken place and that the change would not have occurred without the introduction of the second substance. It is also necessary to demonstrate that the first person could not reasonably have foreseen that the second substance would be introduced and that the change would take place.

TEST 5 - "ESCAPED SUBSTANCES"

This test is intended to exclude from liability persons who would otherwise be liable for the remediation of contaminated land (e.g. as owner) except for the fact that the contaminant in the **'significant pollutant linkage'** has escaped from other land. For this test to apply it is necessary to show that another member of the liability group was responsible for the escape.

TEST 6 - "INTRODUCTION OF PATHWAYS OR RECEPTORS"

In situations where other parties have introduced the pathway or receptor forming part of the significant pollutant linkage, the intention is to exclude from liability persons who had previously introduced the contaminant in question. The introduction of a pathway or receptor may come about through the carrying out of building, engineering or mining operations, or through a change of use in respect of the site or adjoining land. It is necessary to demonstrate that, if the later actions had not been carried out the significant pollutant linkage would not have existed. It should be noted that a local authority that gave planning or building control approval to the works, or change of use, that introduced the pathway or receptor, would not be liable because of the provisions of Test 1 relating to the granting of statutory permissions or licences.

Having applied the tests in respect of the each member of the liability group, and for each identified significant pollutant linkage, the regulating authority has next to decide which, if any, of the members of the liability group should be excluded, either in whole or in part. Having decided whether or not to exclude any members of the liability group the regulator then has to apportion the costs of remediation between the remaining members of the liability group. This is done by reference to the relative periods during which different persons have carried out broadly similar operations; the relative scale of such operations (e.g. by reference to production volumes); the relative areas of land used for the operations; and, a combination of these factors.

Note: Emboldened words are terms used in the legislation or the Statutory Guidance.

Comment

Whilst a developer who has acquired a site for development, and has not continued the polluting activity that caused the pollutant to be present, would normally be a 'Class B' person (i.e. an 'owner' not a 'polluter'), it is possible that development activities could result in the developer becoming a polluter and thus be included in the Class A liability group. This may occur, for example, if engineering works on the site result in the creation of a pathway between contaminant and receptor, such as ground water, and receptors may be introduced in the form of construction workers. Developers therefore need to be mindful of this possibility when preparing their development plans and when appointing consultants and/or contractors.

Appendix 2: Planning Policy Guidance note 3 - Housing

The Government's objectives, as stated in the revised PPG3, include - "The Government intends that everyone should have the opportunity of a decent home." and "To promote more sustainable patterns of development and make better use of previously-developed land, the focus for additional housing should be existing towns and cities." (PPG3, p5).

Among the ways in which local authorities should seek to achieve these objectives are -

* planning to meet the housing requirements of the whole community;

* ensuring the provision of greater diversity in terms of types and tenure of housing;

* seeking to create 'mixed' communities;

* providing sufficient housing land but giving priority to re-using previously-developed land;

* creating more sustainable patterns of development by building in ways which exploit and deliver accessibility to public transport;

* placing the needs of people before cars and reducing the dependence upon cars;

* promoting good design in housing to produce high quality living environments.

The previous policy of 'predicting' the demand for housing over the lifetime of a Unitary Development Plan (UDP) or Structure Plan, and 'providing' land in order to meet that prediction, is to be replaced by 'plan, monitor and manage'. The intention here is to keep the demand for housing land under regular review, with the level of housing provision and its distribution being based on a clear set of policy objectives, linked to measurable indicators of change. This monitoring would then be the basis on which regional planning bodies (RPB's) would formulate and review their housing policies on a not less than five-yearly basis.

Regional Planning Guidance (RPG) and development plans should provide clear guidance as to the location of new housing development, including expected areas of major growth. Structure plans and UDPs should identify growth areas and distribution of housing land at a district level. Local Plans and UDP's should identify sites, and buildings suitable for conversion, at a local level sufficient to meet housing requirements after making allowance for 'windfall' sites.

So far as the allocation of land for housing development is concerned, the presumption is that previously-developed sites (or buildings for re-use or conversion) should be developed before greenfield sites. In following this principle when allocating land for development in local plans and UDP's, local planning authorities should assess the potential and suitability of sites against the following criteria:

- the **availability of previously-developed sites** and empty or under-used buildings and their suitability for housing use;

- the **location and accessibility** of potential development sites to jobs, shops and services by modes other than the car, and the potential for improving such accessibility;

- the **capacity of existing and potential infrastructure**, including public transport, water and sewerage, other utilities and social infrastructure (such as schools and hospitals) to absorb further development and the cost of adding further infrastructure;

- the **ability to build communities** to support new physical and social infrastructure and to provide demand to sustain appropriate local services and facilities; and

- the **physical and environmental constraints on development of land** , including, for example, the level of contamination, stability and flood risk, taking into account that such risk may increase as a result of climate change.

(PPG3, p 13)

This is known as the 'sequential test' approach to the allocation of land for development and the exception to this principle will be where previously-developed sites perform so poorly in relation to these criteria as to preclude their use for housing (within the relevant plan period or phase) before a particular greenfield site.

Windfall sites are those which have not been specifically identified for residential development in the local plan or UDP, because they were in some alternative use, e.g. industry, school or hospital, at the time the relevant plan was prepared. Such sites may comprise a significant proportion of the previously-developed sites becoming available within a local authority's area. Local authorities should seek to make allowance for different types of windfalls, based on past trends, with no allowance being made for greenfield windfalls. It may also be appropriate for authorities to consider reallocating for housing development land that is currently allocated to other uses, such as employment, where that land cannot realistically be taken up for that use during the plan period.

In order to make the best use of available resources, local authorities should avoid the inefficient use of land. This implies increasing development densities beyond the current average of 25 dwellings per hectare. Local authorities should therefore seek to encourage densities of between 30 and 50 dwellings per hectare, and greater intensity of development at places with good public transport accessibility such as city, town, district and local centres or around major transport nodes. Car parking standards at no more than 1.5 off-street spaces per dwelling would be in line with Government policies.

The guidance note recognises that not all development can take place within urban areas but the extent to which development should take place outside existing areas will depend upon the overall need for housing land, the capacity of existing urban areas to accommodate additional housing and the efficiency with which land is developed. Only a limited amount of housing can be expected to be accommodated in expanded villages, for example where it can be demonstrated that additional housing will support local services, such as schools or shops, that would become unviable without some modest growth. Additional housing may also be provided in rural areas to meet specific requirements, such as affordable housing, and to help secure a mixed and balanced community. Rural developments will have to be designed sympathetically and be laid out in keeping with the character of the area.

Comment

A major thrust of this planning policy guidance note is to encourage the re-use of previously used land in preference to developing on Greenfield sites. If the guidance is heeded by local planning authorities, developers are likely to encounter pressure to increase development densities, rather than the other way round as has often been the case in the past. In some cases developers may feel that the move towards reducing car-parking provision will have a detrimental impact on the viability of developments.

Definition of 'previously-developed' land - Previously-developed land is that which is or was occupied by a permanent structure (excluding agricultural or forestry buildings), and associated fixed surface infrastructure. The definition covers the curtilage of the development. Previously-developed land may occur in both built-up and rural settings. The definition includes defence buildings and land used for mineral extraction and waste disposal where provision for restoration has not been made through development control procedures.

(Planning Policy Guidance note 3 - *Housing,* p27)

Note: the definition specifically excludes land and buildings used for agriculture or forestry and previously used land where the remains of any structure or activity have blended into the landscape.